MIDNIGHT TERROR

E. L. VINSON BOWERS

To Courtney

E L Vint Bowers

2021

ISBN: 978-1-66781-357-8 (hardcover)

To Charlotte,

Thanks for your love and encouragement to help make this book a reality.

ELVB

TABLE OF CONTENTS

AUTHOR'S NOTE

This historical novel is a work of fiction, based on facts about the crash of National Airlines Flight 2511 that occurred northwest of Bolivia in Brunswick County, North Carolina on January 6, 1960.

The characters in this novel are mostly fictional, though there are references to actual individuals throughout the book.

Over the last 5 years, I have researched a myriad of sources to include various interviews with local residences who knew of the crash as well as read numerous books and newspaper articles about the turn of events that led up to the crash and the extensive investigation that followed.

It is my opinion that the investigation by the Civil Aeronautics Board was flawed and critical facts were not examined to the fullest extent. Furthermore, with the fierce conflicts that existed between the United States and Cuba at that time, President Eisenhower made key decisions that greatly compromised the outcome of the investigation of this commercial airliner.

From the evidence that I have compiled, NAL Flight 2511 will go down in history as one of the most mysterious and bizarre episodes in the history of aviation.

ACKNOWLEDGEMENT

First and foremost, I am greatly indebted to my good friend, James C. "Jim" High, who shared with me the intriguing story of a horrendous airplane crash that occurred near Whiteville, North Carolina in 1960. Jim's vivid memory of that mysterious disaster always haunted him throughout his outstanding sixty-one-year career as the editor of *The News Reporter*. From his emotional experience witnessing that surreal scene, I was so moved to write about it years later.

I am also grateful for the assistance I received from the dedicated librarians at the Wilmington Public Library, and the staffs at the *Wilmington Star News* and *The News Reporter*. Without their help, I would not have been able to piece together all the important details that solidified the truths of what I believe really happened on that dark stormy night over 60 years ago.

Without question, I am most appreciative for all the support my wife, Charlotte, has given me. I could not have completed this book without her encouragement and her help in editing my manuscript. Many thanks to my good friend, Ed Campbell, for his creative ingenuity and to Meredith Laskovics for her wonderfully designed front cover.

Finally, I thank BookBaby Publishing for their kind assistance in helping publish this fascinating story of the mysterious aviation disaster that took place in eastern North Carolina . . . *MIDNIGHT TERROR*.

INTRODUCTION

As a young teenager, January 6, 1960, was just another cold wintery day. My family lived in southeastern North Carolina beside a beautiful old millpond just outside Whiteville. I spent endless hours growing up outdoors and, during that particular January, the bitter artic winds had pushed the temps so low that the pond had frozen over. There wasn't much to do outside except play with my lab, Rusty.

Looking back, I faintly remember being told about a large airliner crashing between Whiteville and Wilmington. It didn't mean much to me at the time since I wasn't attuned to reading the daily news or watching our black and white TV. However, when I happened to look at the headlines of the local paper, *THE NEWS REPORTER*, I was shocked. It seemed to be a big deal. Did this really happen just a few miles from home?

On that particular January night, just before midnight, National Airlines Flight 2511, a Douglas DC-6B, took off from New York's Idlewild Airport bound south-southwest for Miami carrying 34 passengers and crew. The weather reports indicated that the flight would be facing strong headwinds, heavy cloud coverings and possible rain.

Around one a. m., National Airlines' pilot, Captain Dale Southard, leveled off over Salisbury Maryland at his assigned altitude of 18,000 feet, reaching a cruising speed of approximately 190 mph. As the weather conditions deteriorated, the captain flew solely by instruments. The headwinds were getting stronger and the cloud formations intensifying with intermediate rain; visibility was zero.

At 2:13 a.m. Flight 2511 reported that it was passing over Kinston, North Carolina, 75 miles short of Wilmington. Moments later, the Captain radioed to Airway Traffic Control that Flight 2511 had broken out in the clear passing over Wilmington at 18,000 feet and the plane was finally above the clouds and rain.

At 2:27 a.m., south of Wilmington, Captain Southard reported again to Airway Traffic Control that their estimated arrival to the next ocean check-point would be at 3:02 a.m. Flight 2511 was heading over the Cape Fear River and then to the open Atlantic.

At 2:31 a.m., within a split second, National Airlines Flight 2511 began to rip apart.

On Thursday, the morning of January 7, I rolled out of bed early and headed to our breakfast room table. I sensed that my father was not himself. He greeted me as usual, but acted upset, shaking his head and fidgeting with the paper.

"Son, you might take time and read the paper this morning . . . it's sad what happened a few miles from here the other night . . . it's so hard to understand or imagine," Dad said as he sipped his coffee, staring out of the large bay window overlooking the millpond. Without hesitation, I picked up THE NEWS REPORTER and slowly began to read the headlines. "STILL SEEK TWO BODIES, CAUSE IN 34-DEATH AIRLINER CRASH." I was shocked. So I read it again. I'd never read anything like it before . . . especially the fact that it happened so close to home. I read every word of the gruesome account, but still could not comprehend the magnitude of the tragedy.

"Dad, the paper doesn't say what happened or why. You think someone just shot it down?"

"Son, it will take weeks, probably months to find out what caused the crash. The FBI and other federal authorities have already started investigating according to the paper," Dad said in a calm, but reflective tone. "Earlier this morning, I had occasion to chat with Jim High, who is with the paper as you know, and asked him if he had more insight into the crash. Jim knew a lot . . . a whole lot! He was actually one of the first reporters to witness the crash site just hours after it happened. Jim said it was surreal; earie beyond anything he could have ever imagined. So many mangled bodies; so much twisted metal; so much death."

Fast forward 61 years, I have often thought about whatever happened to that ill-fated National Airliner that crashed near my hometown. The memories I have are still vivid asking my father about that horrible crash so many years ago.

In 2016, I read an article by Ben Steelman with the *WILMINGTON STAR NEWS*. He wrote that in the final Civil Aeronautics Board report that it ruled out weather, technical problems, human error, and other factors in the crash, but settled on the fact that a passenger had blown up the plane. Why did the investigation simply stop there? Furthermore, are there any connections to a mysterious crash of another National Airlines flight that had gone down in the Gulf of Mexico in another apparent bombing just two months earlier?

Steelman's article stirred my interest in this mystery. Weeks later, I spent the day at the Wilmington Public Library to compile more details of what might have happened at the time of the crash. However, the trove of information that I found on the internet pushed me over the top. The more I dug into the facts that surrounded this crash, the more I was convinced that there had been a deliberate governmental cover up to hide the real truth that caused the crash of Flight 2511. I am convinced that the CIA, the Miami Mafia, and Fidel Castro all had a hand in the many twists and turns that lead up to this horrible plane crash that still remains an UNSOLVED AVIATION MYSTERY AND THE WORST AIR DESASTER EVER RECORDED IN SOUTHEASTERN NORTH CAROLINA.

I

NEW YORK GETAWAY

NEW YORK, NEW YORK

D ecember 12, 1958, was a brisk winter day in Midtown. The joyous season was at full tilt with a multitude of colorful lights flashing at every turn. The hustle and bustle of New York City added excitement to the spirit of the Christmas season. Horns were blaring, yellow cabs were zipping by and the evening was fast approaching. Along the crowded sidewalk on 52nd street, Julian and Bridget, donned in top coats, walked hurriedly hand-in- hand toward their favorite New York restaurant, The 21 Club.

"Welcome Mr. and Mrs. Frank. How are you tonight," the maître de' asked with a familiar tone.

"Very well, Charles, thank you"

"Your table is ready . . . right this way," gestured Charles, dressed in his dark suit and tie.

The starched white table cloth featured two red roses in a tall glass vase. After they were seated, the waiter placed menus on their table and asked if they would like to have a cocktail.

"Yes, my wife and I would like a dry martini, please."

"Certainly," the waiter replied.

One of the most famous bars and restaurants in New York dating back to the 1930's, this legendary club featured dining at its finest. As one peruses the menu of American classics and enjoys the elegant setting, an interesting feature in the room are the whimsical "toys" suspended from the ceiling. These unique gifts were given by famous celebrities, sports stars and even presidents over the years.

"Bridget, you are beautiful tonight wearing your new pearl necklace," Julian said staring into his wife's blue eyes.

"Thank you dear," Bridget replied as she gently leaned her head to one side.

"Hope you found the hotel accommodations in good order."

"Yes, the room at the Warwick is very nice. My drive in from Westport went well; thankfully there was very little traffic this morning. I arrived in town early enough today to get settled. Just before I left the room, I called the sitter at home and she said the children are doing fine and all is quiet for the moment," Bridget said with a big smile.

"Wonderful!"

They raised their glasses and lightly tapped them together. As they gazed into each other's eyes for a moment, the lights in the room dimmed and soft jazz played in the background. The night was special. It was their sixth wedding anniversary and they were staying in the City overnight.

Julian, a handsome 33-year-old with light brown hair and a muscular build, was an aspiring attorney in Manhattan. He was a high-energy individual, destined for great success. He grew up in Trenton under strict discipline by his mother who was a local high school English teacher. His father, however, died early from a severe heart attack leaving a modest pension for his family from the New Jersey Railroad fund.

Even though Julian's early years were tough, he had a wealth of friends and was academically gifted. He worked odd jobs all through school to help his mother financially and won a scholarship to

Columbia University. Julian was very focused and determined to succeed. He graduated from law school years later and joined a large New
York law firm for several years before he decided to start his own
practice.

"Dear, have you decided on what you might want to eat tonight?"
Julian asked as he looked the menu over. "Get anything you wish. We
are celebrating."

"I'm in the mood for a good medium-rare filet, thanks." Bridget
replied glancing up at Julian with a smile.

"I'll probably do the same." Julian closed his menu inside of the
leather folder and looked up at the server dressed in a white starched
jacket.

During their meal, they talked about family and what Santa gifts
they both had in mind for the children.

"Let's take time to walk down 5th Avenue tomorrow. I want to drop
in several shops, especially the one I modeled for years ago . . . want
to see what's new." Bridget suggested.

"Great idea," Julian agreed.

Bridget had been a successful New York fashion model and worked
for some of the top agencies in Manhattan. She was tall, slender, and
wore her honey-colored hair to her shoulders. She grew up in an afflu-
ent neighborhood in Philadelphia and was loved by her peers. She
had a winning personality and was an accomplished tennis player.
Bridget attended Princeton Day School in New Jersey her last two
years of high school. She had her sights set on a career in the fashion
world, and later completed a rigorous stint at one of the most presti-
gious modeling schools in New York. After just a few years working
as a model on 5th Avenue, Bridget met the love of her life at a New York
City charity fundraiser party. A whirlwind courtship followed, and
Bridget and Julian were soon married.

Completing their delicious dinner, Julian suggested that they ease
into the elegant 21 Club bar for a celebratory drink. The setting was
warm and inviting with lights turned down low. The long, polished
mahogany bar was curved at one end with matching dark brown

leather stools. Behind the bar was a massive decorative mirror with glass shelving lined with the finest whiskies. As the Franks positioned themselves at the bar, they were greeted by a world renowned bartender with a distinct British accent, Colin Smith. "What is the pleasure of the lady tonight?" Colin asked as he leaned to Bridget.

"I think we would like two White-Russians . . . thank you." Julian said with pride.

"Certainly."

Their relaxing conversation with Colin was delightful as they romanced their wonderful cocktail. Looking at his watch, Julian suggested to Bridget that they might retrieve their coats. He had a special surprise for her.

"Dear, let's grab a cab and head to Bemelmans Bar . . . you always wanted to go to Bemelmans to see the famous murals, and listen to some soft jazz. So tonight we are going!"

"That sounds fabulous!"

As they arrived at The Carlyle Hotel on the Upper East Side, they were ushered through the elegant white marble lobby, and over to the intimate, dimly-lit iconic bar as the famous pianist, Earl Rose, was performing one of his favorite songs. After they were seated, Julian ordered a round of Martinis. As the soft jazz pulled them into a romantic mood, Bridget could not keep her eyes off the magnificent murals by the "Madeline" illustrator Ludwig Bemelman. The colorful illustrations were everywhere.

"Julian, this elegant bar has such an incredible atmosphere . . . it is so endearing, so New York!"

"Dear, I totally agree . . . I really love the jazz."

As midnight approached, Julian suggested that they might call it a night, it was getting late.

After a short ride back to the Warwick Hotel, Julian and Bridget were ready to turn in for the evening. They both spoke fondly of the special time they had together that night. It was a time they would reflect on for the coming years.

The Warwick Hotel, built in 1926 by William Hurst, has been a landmark in Midtown for years. It is on the corner of 65 W 54th Street and is a magnificent luxury hotel with a gold plated entry-way leading into a white marble reception area. Many celebrities like the Beatles, Elvis Presley, Cary Grant, Elizabeth Taylor and many others stayed at the Warwick because of its impeccable service and fabulous accommodations.

After a fun two day getaway, the Franks were back in Westport and settling into their normal routine. Bridget was focused on the children's school work and activities, while Julian was up before dawn taking the commuter train to his office on 47th street in the City. Walking five blocks from Grand Central, he would take the elevator to the 16th floor to his modest, but beautifully appointed office. The polished oak paneling opened up to floor-to-ceiling windows that faced east. On sunny days, his view of Manhattan was breathtaking.

As he slipped off his top coat and removed his hat entering the office, Julian greeted his assistant, Miss Jefferies, who was busy typing a mortgage loan document.

"Good morning, Miss Jefferies, did you and your boyfriend go to the outdoor concert in Central Park this weekend?" Julian asked.

"Yes, Julian, we had a blast! Stayed out until about 3 a. m. Did you and Bridget celebrate your anniversary in the City? Miss Jefferies inquired.

"Yes, we had a great time … any appointments today or calls I need to return?"

"Yes, Mr. Wilson called and asked for you to call him back this morning. Also, you have a closing set for three this afternoon."

"Thanks."

Julian was very fortunate to have Miss Jefferies, a skilled paralegal who knew the business. Her role was critical to Julian's success as an attorney just starting a new practice. She would make sure Julian's critical deadlines were kept, make his appointments for him, and help with the editing and filing of his legal documents. They would work together on almost every case … start to finish.

The first year that Julian's practice was open, his client list was limited and his billings modest. He was able to retain some of his clients from his old firm, and began to get some referrals from mortgage brokers. Julian's network of friends in the banking and legal business had been of great help to him. He took the advice of others and attended numerous business functions, but he quickly found out that the competition in the legal world was fierce. The large, well-established New York firms were well connected and controlled most of the mortgage business that Julian was trying to penetrate.

Julian knew he could succeed . . . it was just a matter of time.

II

SOUTHERN LIVING

WHITEVILLE, NORTH CAROLINA

A s the sleek Atlantic Coast Line train eased to a halt at the Vineland station in the quaint southern town of Whiteville, North Carolina, Jay Richardson opened the gold shell of his watch and found the train on time. He glanced out the window and spotted his farm manager, Will Jones, standing in the crowd. Turning to his bride, Jackie, he gently kissed her on the cheek and said, "Dear, we're home."

They had just returned from a holiday visit with Jackie's family in Trenton, New Jersey. It was the first of January, 1960, and Jay was eager to get back to the farm.

Sporting a blue blazer and a colorful silk square tucked in his breast pocket, Jay stood 6' 2" with sandy colored hair and steal blue eyes. He was athletic and an avid hunter. Jay had spent his life working on the family farm and loved it. After his four years at State College, he returned home and worked tirelessly to expand the tobacco and cattle operations that his father had set in motion back in the early 1930's.

Will had gotten to the train station early the day of their return from New Jersey and was leaning against the family's new Buick sedan, smoking a cigarette. As a farm manager, Will was an expert at his trade. He had no formal education, but knew from years of experience how to produce an excellent tobacco crop year after year. Will was an outdoorsman as well and if he wasn't working in the fields with the hired hands on a typical day, he was floating down the Waccamaw River in his dugout canoe fishing for large-mouth bass and blue gills.

"Will, it is so nice of you to meet us . . . it's been a long trip," Jackie said as she greeted him stepping from the wooden train platform wearing a beautiful long- black button-down coat and tall black leather boots.

"It's my pleasure. I know you had a good time . . . it's been quiet here, thankfully," Will said as he reached out and assisted Jackie with her handbags.

After a short drive south of Whiteville, Will came in view of the Richardson property lined with white fences and rolling pastures along the roadway. He started decelerating and turned left off Highway 130 on a pine-straw lane marked by tall brick columns. Large pin oaks canopied the long lane leading up to the Richardson's white two-story brick home, which was originally the main office of a giant sawmill back in the early 1920's.

The vast farm land that surrounded the Richardson home was once owned by Jackson Brothers Lumber Company out of Delaware. Employing over 500 men, the huge complex functioned as an independent village, called Brunswick. The massive sawmill provided company housing for all its employees, including utilities, and a well-stocked commissary. During a typical day, steam locomotives muscled train-loads of pine logs to the mill from the surrounding five counties.

The huge logs were debarked, sorted and run through screaming circular saws that bellowed clouds of sawdust over the tree-lined village. The sweet aroma of pine sap filled the air from stacks of rough-cut lumber that covered acres and acres of land surrounding the small community.

Jay Richardson's parents, Ernest and Julia, were one of the many families who moved to Brunswick when the mill was first built. Ernest managed the company commissary up until the Great Depression hit. Within a couple of years, Jay's father acquired the land around the old mill site and a sizable acreage of farmland. Times were hard back then, but Ernest believed that hard work paid off over time.

When Jay and Jackie arrival at their home, Blanche Nance, their devoted maid, stepped from the kitchen door and greeted the young couple with a giant smile and a big hug. "So glad you'll made it back safely. We missed you," Blanche said with animation wearing a white starched apron over her navy blue dress.

"Blanche, we sure missed you too," Jackie replied. "I trust you and your family enjoyed the holidays."

"Oh yes. Just a nice time with family . . . how was your trip to Trenton?"

"We had a great time. New Jersey is cold and drab this time of year as you can imagine, but my family is well, except for Dad who is in poor health. I think Jay had fun meeting everyone, and especially, enjoyed the home cooked Italian food and the fabulous wines from the old country. As you can imagine, my mama is a good Italian cook and Jay loved all her Italian dishes . . . spaghetti and meatballs, lasagna and several others."

"He probably gained a few pounds eating all those pasta dishes," Blanche said smiling.

"I'm sure he did."

"How was your brother, Vinnie, doing?" inquired Blanche.

"He's fine...Jay spent a lot of time talking with him about our family business. Vinnie shared a few incites of the iron-fist operation that papa started years ago. They're in the trucking business . . . hauling garbage from New York City to several landfills. It's a rough and dirty business . . . my brother handles the hiring and firing of the drivers, and he can be a little too hard on the guys, I think."

Close-net, secretive, and wealthy best described her family...The Genovese. Jackie's father, Vito, adored his only beautiful daughter, Jackie, but did not extend the same warmth to her husband, Jay, who was a die-hard southerner. Vito, who was hardened to the core, did not befriend Jay because he did not have Italian blood running though his veins or a single Sicilian bone in his body. However, that did not stop Jay from having an engaging time with all the younger Genovese brothers, cousins and nephews. From Jay's point of view, the Genovese had to be Mafia, without question . . . they drove black Fleetwood Cadillacs with white-wall tires, wore gold chains, fancy fedoras, and still spoke Italian when they greeted each other. However, brother Vinnie phrased it a little differently to Jay . . . the family controls the lucrative refuse disposal business in the New Jersey/New York area and we challenge anybody who messes with us!

After Jay and Will unloaded the light blue Buick sedan and carried all the luggage and bags inside, the two grabbed a beer and sat down in the living room to discuss farm matters. The farms had become quite sizable over the years and Will played a key role in its success.

Starting with approximately 125 acres back in 1932, Jay's father, Ernest, formed a share-cropper agreement with three devoted tenant farmers . . . Lonnza McCallister, his brother, Theodore McCallister, and Quincy Rives. These men plowed the fields with long-eared mules and small Farmall tractors day in and day out during the hot, sweltering summer months. Times back then were hard, demanding, and back-breaking. Most years the crops sold well at harvest time, but some years were disastrous due to heavy rains and insects.

Fast forward a quarter of a century, Jay and Will grew the operation to incorporate a thousand acres under cultivation, using the latest designed equipment to cultivate and harvest tobacco, as well as numerous grains like soybeans, corn and oats. Tobacco was the big cash crop that drove the economy in the Whiteville area and the whole town benefited from it. Jay knew the importance of growing tobacco each and every year, but his love was his cattle. The Richardson homestead was graced with long white fencing and green pastures around its perimeter where Jay's herd of purebred Herefords were kept in close view.

The very next morning after the Richardsons returned from holiday, Jackie was in the kitchen.

"Miss Jackie . . . want to see what I'm cooking for you and Mr. Jay for dinner?"

"Oh, Blanche, there is nothing more enjoyable than coming home and watching you prepare your delicious southern food. From my Italian background, this is all new to me. I'm from a world of pastas, heavy sauces and cured meats. You have shown me ways of cooking that I did not imagine. I especially love how you use your black skillet to make corn bread, southern fried chicken, and collard greens."

While Jackie was busy in the kitchen shadowing Blanche, Jay had been up since daybreak looking over the farm. It was around eight o'clock when he returned home for breakfast, slipping off his muddy boots.

"Hi dear, are you taking some pointers from the master cook?"

"You know I am," Jackie replied, smiling. "Blanche is preparing dinner and she is showing me how to make an apple pie from scratch. I marvel at how she rolls the dough and prepares the pie crust . . . she is wonderful. Oh, I forgot to ask if you found everything in order on the farm."

"Yes, everything appears to be in good order . . . later, I'm going to walk through the pasture and look over the herd and check on the young calves."

"If I'm unpacked then, I'd like to walk with you . . . I really enjoy seeing the young calves romping and playing in the pasture," Jackie exclaimed.

"Of course. Let's plan on that," Jay replied, pleased.

After a hearty breakfast, Jay headed upstairs to his spacious office in their home. Sorting through the stack of mail that had accumulated over the holiday, he began to reflect on their recent trip to Jackie's home in New Jersey. Jay was always touched at how Jackie's family, being Italian, was so close and caring to each other. It meant a lot to him. Glancing at his favorite framed picture of his bride on his desk, he fondly remembered the special time they had in Wilmington years ago. Watching a beautiful sunset over the Cape Fear River at a riverfront restaurant on Princess Street in the Port City, they shared endearing stories of their past, as well as a few laughs as they enjoyed a splendid bottle of Pinot Noir with their dinner. That night Jay knew she was the one!

Before the sun slipped behind the tall pin oaks in their yard, Jay and Jackie slipped into their boots and heavy coats and headed out the back gate. A cool chilling breeze from the north blew across the rolling pastures. After a short walk, they approached the cattle that were chomping on the bales of hay placed in the pasture. The couple did not frighten the white-faced cows that stared at them with a sense of approval. Jackie pointed out the three-month-old frisky calves with delight. As for Jay, he was truly enjoying the beautiful tranquil moment admiring his prized herd. He could not forget the time when he was 6 years old when his father introduced him to a two-day-old calf . . . the big-eyed calf with wobbly legs just stood there and did not flinch when Jay touched its face. At that moment, Jay became a true cattleman.

As the couple walked back to their home, Jackie suggested to Jay, "Love, would you be interested in riding over to Woodbridge in the next couple of days? I have a new sisal rug for the master bedroom I would like to try."

"You read my mind. I'll look at my calendar. I want to go quail hunting at the plantation as well. I'd love for you to join me on the hunt if you would like."

"That's a date!" Jackie replied with a big smile.

III

ZAPPIA'S TAVERN

TRENTON, NEW JERSEY

Riding the commuter train back home after work each night, Julian had time to think and reflect. It was a time for him to just relax and be quiet; no phone calls or interruptions. His immediate thoughts were always about money . . . how to make more and how to pay current monthly bills. He put long hours in at the office, but he just couldn't get ahead. He felt there had to be a better way to make extra cash on the side; non-reportable cash, cash that could get him out of his financial dilemma. He knew for sure that he couldn't borrow from his personal bank because his wife would have to co-sign, and that would never work. Also, he knew he could not ask one of his wealthy clients to lend him thousands of dollars; that would be unprofessional.

As he sat quietly in his seat, listening to the sounds of the commuter train making its way down the tracks and watching the street lights rapidly pass by his window, Julian's mind drifted back to his youth growing up in New Jersey when times were simpler. Those days you only spent the little money you had and no more.

As Julian thought about his old buddies, the name of a friend came to mind who he ran with some in Trenton when he was in high school. His old classmate was always in trouble with the law, but he had made a lot of money over the years. Julian remembered that his friend's family had connections . . . maybe not the most ethical, but Julian felt he was pinned against the wall. Maybe it was time to call his old friend, Ricky Russo. Everyone back then called him Fats.

Before Julian knew it, the commuter train slowed to a halt and the doors opened at the Westport station. He had had a long day and most nights he would arrive home after his family had eaten dinner. Normally, he only had time to briefly visit with his children before they were ushered to bed. Julian wanted things to be different. He hoped he could change things and figure out a way to get out of the miserable financial rut he had gotten himself into. He was determined to do something about it.

"Sorry I got home later than normal, I had to complete a document for one of my best clients. Thankfully, Miss Jefferies had everything prepared for me to review," Julian said as he fixed himself a Scotch.

"I understand, dear. The children had a fun day playing in the snow with friends and by dark, they were exhausted, ready for bed," Bridget shared, hugging Julian.

"I'm so glad it's the weekend. Is there anything special you would like to do tomorrow?" Julian said, kissing Bridget.

"After breakfast, let's take the kids to the park so they can ice skate and maybe take in an afternoon movie. Sound good?" Bridget suggested.

"I'm in . . . just let me sleep 'til nine tomorrow. I'll help you fix breakfast like we always do on Saturday and we'll head out," Julian suggested as he took a sip of his drink.

Bridget was a good mom. She had adjusted to married life, as well as to the young children's rigorous daily schedule. She missed her modeling days and all the beautiful clothes from the top designers, but she was happy. However, over the last year, she began noticing that Julian had changed . . . something was different. Something was occupying his thoughts at times, and he would just say he had a lot of pressing deals at work.

The Franks lived in an attractive two-story home in one of the oldest established neighborhoods in Westport, and were regulars at the local country club. Bridget had a tennis group she played with every week, weather permitting, while Julian spent his time playing cards with his buddies when he wasn't with the family on the weekends. He was a whiz at cards... especially poker. From time-to-time, Julian would get so enthralled at the card table, if he won, he could be obnoxious... really obnoxious. He was known as a boastful fella, one who tended to brag a little too much.

Some days at the poker table, Julian took delight in telling the guys about seeing some young good-looking "broad" at lunch on 5th Avenue or overhearing the inside scoop on a hot stock that was now trading on Wall Street. His buddies would roll their eyes, laugh, and then continue playing cards. One time Julian told the story of catching a fly ball in center field at Yankee Stadium in his giant beer cup ... everybody around him got drenched.

On the surface, life for the Frank family seemed very good. They had a core of close friends, were sociably active in the community and lived the all-American dream. However, that was the furthest thing from the truth. Julian's lavish life-style far exceeded his modest income as a struggling attorney in the City. Julian was in debt up to his ears. He had maxed his credit cards and home equity line. Julian was only able to pay the minimums at best on his current bills. Julian never told his wife his true financial difficulties. As far as Julian knew, Bridget never had a clue of her husband's indebtedness or his financial crisis. But Julian was dead wrong... sadly, Bridget knew what was going on. She knew they were in serious financial trouble. She had seen the credit card bills, minimum payments and past due notices. However, Julian had a temper and Bridget had yet to breach the subject.

The very next week, Julian called his old school classmate, Ricky Russo, and asked him if he had time to meet... it was important. Ricky agreed and suggested Zappia's Tavern in the Down Neck community of Trenton, New Jersey. The thriving blue-collar neighborhood had been a popular hangout for crime figures for decades and Ricky lived there. Ricky was drinking a beer and smoking a cigarette in the back booth of the dark-paneled restaurant when Julian arrived. Ricky raised his hand and signaled Julian to join him. Ricky, wearing a gold chain around his neck, was bald, overweight and had tattoos down his left arm.

Ricky was known by the cops. He had continual run-ins with the law and numerous arrests ranging from gambling, extortion and bribery to name a few. He had a bad reputation to say the least.

"How the hell are you doing old boy," Ricky said sharing a big smile and a strong handshake.

"Doing pretty well, Ricky. It's been years since I've seen you . . . 12 years at least."

"Let me buy you a beer. You look like you could use a good drink!" Ricky said staring at Julian.

"Thanks anyway, I've got to get back to the office later today," Julian explained as he relaxed his tie and unbuttoned the top of his shirt.

"You being a big-shot lawyer in the City, what the hell are you wanting to talk to me for anyway? Do the Fed's have something on me again . . . those lousy sons-of-bitches," Ricky said as he rolled his eyes and took another sip of his Pabst Blue Ribbon beer.

"No Ricky. Absolutely not. I don't deal with those guys." Julian said nervously rubbing his face. "I need your help . . . I really do, man,"

"What is it?" Ricky stared at Julian with inquisitive eyes.

"Well . . ."

As they talked, Julian told Ricky of the financial crunch that he was in and he needed help. Ricky could see that Julian was sincere and troubled. Julian did his best to make his point of urgency and that he needed cash as soon as possible. Ricky told Julian that he would talk with the Family and see what could be done.

After an hour of reminiscing about old high school classmates and funny pranks they instigated, Julian thanked Ricky sincerely for his time, shook hands and left.

Ricky Russo was a trusted "wise-guy" with ties to one of the most powerful crime families in New Jersey and New York, the Gambino family. Ricky felt sure that Julian Frank could get the money. Julian's roots were from New Jersey, he was a hard worker, smart with a law degree and, most importantly, the Gambino family could always use a good attorney at the right price.

With Julian's pressing predicament, the Gambino godfather reluctantly agreed to advance Julian the cash he requested, with one agreement . . . Julian must do as he was told. When one receives money from the Family, one must pay it back as agreed . . . no exceptions.

Some of the many lucrative criminal ventures that the Gambino family dealt in were loan-sharking and fraudulent mortgage deals. Their loan scams were designed to fulfill a need for individuals with poor credit or ones who needed cash immediately. The Gambino group needed a lawyer in the mix and Julian Frank would be a perfect fit to manipulate the legal angles.

After a week had passed, Ricky made the call to Julian and told him to meet him at the same Italian tavern in Jersey at noon. Ricky wanted to give Julian the good news in person, and reiterate the agreement that the Family required upon loaning money to someone. You must pay the Family back as agreed . . . no exceptions.

After Julian sat down in the back booth at Zappia's, Ricky looked into Julian's eyes and said with conviction, "Old pal, I've worked it all out and you'll get the money you've asked for. Now, don't disappoint me. Do everything you are asked, and everything will be OK."

"It's a deal," Julian said hastily, shaking Ricky's hand."

Thousands of dollars poured into Julian's business account from an untraceable source the very next week. Within a few days, his friend Ricky called once again.

"Julian, did you get the money?" Ricky asked.

"Yes, thanks!" Julian said with guarded excitement. The exact amount of cash Julian had requested had arrived on time by wire transfer. Being a New York licensed attorney, Julian was trying to think through the legal aspects of what he had gotten into. He now realized that he was tied to the underworld and they owned him.

Ricky mentioned to Julian that someone would be in touch with him soon. The Gambino family needed some legal matters handled in Jersey and New York, as well as Florida. They were confident that Julian would expedite the legal aspects of the transactions.

When Julian hung up the phone from Ricky's riveting conversation, Julian knew he was trapped, but he had no choice. He had to have the money, he was financially stretched out, but he felt certain that over time he could repay the money in full as agreed. He was sure of that.

By early spring of 1959, Julian had paid off all his pressing financial obligations, and even salted away a few extra dollars. At times, Julian would brag about his investments to his close friends and tell what a shrewd investor he had been lately. He became brash, even cocky at times. Bridget was thankful of her husband's success and that their financial worries seemed to have gone away.

"Julian, this sure has been an exceptionally good year for you!" Bridget said with a big smile.

"Yes, dear. Things have really turned around for me. I'm partnering with some savvy businessmen who have helped me develop several key lucrative accounts," Julian replied pushing his chest out, staring into space. "These men need my legal expertise and it's been a good fit. Everything is going well."

At his office, Julian kept secret files of the illegal documents that the Gambino's had required him to expedite. He did not breathe a word to his legal assistant, Miss Jefferies, about his dealings with his new partners. Everything with the Mafia was kept in his desk under lock and key.

Almost every month, the Gambino organization would have Julian prepare contracts that had excessive interest rates and various strict stipulations. These transactions were illegal from the start, and violated all code of ethics that Julian had sworn to uphold as a licensed attorney. To make matters worse, Julian was only licensed in New York, not in New Jersey or Florida.

Julian had committed himself to a world of corruption.

IV

WOODBRIDGE PLANTATION

JANUARY 5, 1960
BRUNSWICK COUNTY, NORTH CAROLINA

The cool breezes of January were blowing across the landscape at Woodbridge Plantation. Temps were dropping down into the low 30's at night, but by midday, it was back up to the upper 50's. Scattered white clouds graced the light blue sky. By mid-morning Jay was sitting on the side porch with his feet propped up on the wooden railing sipping his second cup of coffee. He had been up since dawn, and was taking a break having just finished his chores on the farm.

As the clouds gave way to the bright sun coming up from the east, Jackie rounded the porch wearing a long terrycloth robe and leaned over to kiss Jay. She had been in the kitchen helping Blanche prepare breakfast.

"Jay, breakfast is served, my love . . . Blanche has put everything on the breakfast table," Jackie said as she tightened her white robe.

"Thanks. I was hoping you were coming to get me for breakfast. I'm really hungry," Jay said taking his cowboy hat off, placing it in the chair.

"Are we still going quail hunting today . . . you think the weather will work in our favor?" Jackie asked in a spirited manner.

"Yes, dear . . . I'm counting on it. It appears today should be good for hunting," Jay said reassuringly. "The forecast calls for possible rain late this afternoon, but that want interfere with our hunt."

Jay had always wanted a large tract of land not too far from Whiteville to create a lasting quail preserve; it was his passion. After several years, a friend of his contacted him about property adjacent to the massive Green Swamp that lies in both Brunswick and Columbus counties. The tract was comprised of an old antebellum plantation house surrounded by giant live oaks and approximately 800 acres of good farmland. The old wooden two-story home place was modest and had a wraparound porch and, of course, was in dire need of repair. It was perfect for Jay and Jackie and a favorite getaway on most weekends.

After a hearty breakfast, Jay headed down to the old stable and met James, the hunt master. As they were getting the hunt wagon loaded with shot guns, ammo, bird dogs and ample refreshments, Jackie arrived dressed in her Barber hunting attire with a dark green wool scarf, leather gloves and boots.

"Honey, I've already saddled your horse. If you want to go ahead and mount, I will get my horse ready and we will be off," Jay said to Jackie as she fastened her helmet securely.

The fertile rolling farmland was ideal for growing millet, corn, and other hardy grains to sustain a good quail population. The fields were divided into ten acre plots with wide paths for the horses and hunt wagon to maneuver. One practice that the hunt master lived by was not to shoot more than two or three quail out of a covey at a given time. By following this simple rule, the quail population would flourish and there would be plenty of quail the following year.

As the hunt party assembled, James asked for everyone to follow him as he headed down a long winding lane through the southern part of the farm. Trailing behind James on his horse was the rickety mule wagon driven by one of the young dog trainers. Following the wagon, Jay and Jackie rode side by side on their quarter horses. After a short time, the hunt party arrived at an endless wire grass field bordered by scattered long-leaf pines and river oaks.

Wearing a tweed cap, a dark green corduroy jacket and snake boots, James pulled the reins to turn his horse around to face the hunt party and said, "Just as a reminder folks, when I bring my horse to a complete stop and raise my hat, everyone needs to be very quiet because the dogs have pointed!"

While they were stopped, the young dog trainer opened the dog box at the rear of the wooden hunt wagon and two of the finest hunting dogs in the county jumped to the ground. The beautiful English Pointers circled the hunt party twice and off they flew, jumping over the tall grasses in graceful leaps.

At that time, Jay advanced his horse beside James while Jackie stayed back beside the burnt red hunt wagon. She chose to just watch the hunt that day because the wind chill had become a factor.

As the hunt party slowly maneuvered through the tall grass fields, it wasn't long before James came to a complete stop and raised his hat signaling a covey of quail had been found. The lead English Pointer hoisted his tail straight up, while the second dog "honored" the point, holding perfectly still in its tracks.

Jay and James dismounted, pulled their 16-gauge shot guns from their sheaths and carefully moved toward the bird dogs. With their guns readied, the quail suddenly erupted from the thicket of wire grass making a thunderous roar. Shots were fired, and feathers drifted to the ground.

"Great shot, Jay . . ." James shouted out. "Man, you got doubles!"

"Thanks," Jay answered with a big grin. "How did you do, James"

"Only hit one, sir . . . That sure was a large covey!"

With their heart beats still racing, the hunters watched enthusiastically as the dogs retrieved the fallen birds and presented the "bobwhites" to the hunt master. After the dogs placed the birds at James' feet, he gave them a treat, patting them on their heads.

"It doesn't get any better than this, James," Jay said with pride as he walked over to check on Jackie. As Jay approached Jackie's horse, she exclaimed, "You guys are good shots, I must say."

"Thanks dear. You are kind to say that, but it's from a lot of practice over the years and a little bit of luck!" Jay shared.

For the next hour or so, the men hunted and the wagon train followed. Half way through the hunt, everyone took a break and enjoyed the refreshments stored in the back of the old wagon . . . pimento cheese sandwiches, chocolate-chip cookies and soft drinks.

It wasn't long before Jay spoke in a commanding voice, sitting high in his saddle, "If all are in agreement, let's head in for the day folks. We've had a good hunt!"

As the caravan returned to the old stable, Jay pulled out a silver engraved flask filled with Irish whiskey and passed it around to fill everyone's jigger. This was an old southern tradition that Jay's dad had always enjoyed. As everyone raised their jiggers at the same time, Jay said, "James, thanks for a successful and safe hunt! You are a master sportsman!"

Looking over the colorful quail placed on a wooded table in the barn, Jay said, "James, please have four birds cleaned and given to Blanche so they can be prepared for our dinner tonight. And, I want you to divide the remaining nine birds among you and the young trainers who have been assisting us."

"Mr. Jay, thank you . . . we will certainly enjoy them."

Jay reached for Jackie's hand, and asked, "Honey, I hope you have had fun this afternoon?"

"Oh yes, dear, I really enjoyed watching the bird dogs crisscrossing through the fields in pursuit of the quail, and how the dogs "locked-up" the second a covey was spotted. It sure was fun to watch." Jackie replied enthusiastically.

"Jackie, if you like, let's head up to the house and freshen up a bit. I need to relax for a while and I'm sure you do too!"

"Great idea, I'm still trying to get my land legs back from riding the horse this afternoon," Jackie said as they were leaving the old barn.

Just before sunset, dinner was served by candle light in the yellow pine dining room as light rain began crossing the dark brown fields. Jackie was very pleased with the selection of Pinot Noir that Jay had chosen to go with the smothered quail entrée.

As Blanche entered the dining room, Jackie exclaimed, "Blanche, you have once again outdone herself. The meal is delicious!"

"I am so glad . . . Y'all take your time and enjoy!" Blanche said with a kind smile.

After they finished the wonderful meal, Jackie excused herself and went into the kitchen to help Blanche, while Jay eased out on the porch to smoke his favorite Cuban cigar. The outdoor breeze was refreshing to him and he began reflecting on the fun time they had quail hunting earlier that day. Watching the dogs work was especially pleasing to Jay. James knew his business when it came to quail hunting.

It wasn't long before Jackie stepped out on the porch and sat beside Jay to enjoy the calmness of the cool night. "Love, I think I'm ready for bed . . . how about you dear?" Jackie said softly as she watch the light rain in the distance.

Jay put his cigar out in the astray beside him and turned to Jackie, "I'm ready too dear . . . It's been a great day. Hope we don't get a lot of rain out of the winter storm tonight."

They both stood and headed upstairs.

V

IDLEWILD
INTERNATIONAL AIRPORT

JANUARY 5, 1960
NEW YORK, NEW YORK

T he windshield wipers could hardly keep up with the blinding rain as Bridget fought to keep her new silver Cadillac sedan in her lane. Her high-beams helped cut through the stormy night. Ahead, Bridget could finally see the bright glow of the huge Idlewild International Airport lighting up the sky as she made the final turn to the National Airlines Terminal. She pulled up to the loading area, stopped her car and turned to Julian.

"Do you really have to go to Miami tonight? Is it that important, Julian? It is such a horrible night to fly," Bridget said emotionally. "I am so worried; I really am."

"Love, I understand. I know the weather is bad and I do share your concern. I wish I could postpone this trip as well. You know how much I hate to fly, especially in bad weather. However, I have no choice. I have put this meeting off twice. This meeting is extremely important tomorrow and I can't miss it," Julian stated leaning over, putting his hand gently on Bridget's shoulder. "Honey, give me a moment so I can get my bag out of the trunk."

Bridget watched him as he placed his luggage on the sidewalk and then got back into the front seat.

"I love you, dear," Julian said as he leaned over and kissed Bridget goodbye. "I will call you as soon as I land in Miami . . . I promise."

"I love you too . . . please be safe," Bridget said sadly as she watched Julian ease out of the passenger seat and grab his bag on the sidewalk and disappear into the busy terminal.

Bridget put her head on the steering wheel and began crying. She felt faint and sick to her stomach. She sensed that Julian was not himself . . . his mind was somewhere else. Even the children sensed something was wrong with their father. Was it something from work, a legal matter, or possibly someone was pressuring him about one of his business dealings? Bridget had noticed that since his practice was finally doing well and he was financially secure, Julian was still not himself. He had a hard time relaxing and was short tempered at times. What could it be? Bridget was very concerned. What was so important about this rushed trip to Miami? Why tonight?

Julian worked his way to the counter, placed his large bag on the scales, and slid his credentials toward the ticket agent. Quickly, the agent made eye contact with him, looked up his flight, printed his boarding pass, and tagged his bag. Julian thanked her and began to proceed to the departure gate.

As he made his way down a long corridor, a big-belled man dressed in black and wearing dark glasses stepped in front of Julian and said in a demanding voice, "Mr. Frank, step over here and stay quiet. Take this and read the note, you hear."

As soon as the man shoved the blue travel bag into Julian's stomach, and Julian grabbed it, the man dressed in black disappeared into the crowd.

"Hey! Hey you! Come back here, dammit!" Julian shouted.

For a moment, Julian just stood there, lost for words. He dropped the blue bag on the floor and tore open the note. It was simple and to the point . . . 'Keep this travel bag with you at all times on the plane, or Bridget will be in serious danger for her life. Someone will be waiting for you at the Miami airport.'

Reading the note a second time, Julian knew more than ever that what Ricky Russo had told him had come true. Julian could not get out of his head the meeting he had with Ricky the week before. He could not forget his harsh, curt words. Julian was scared to death.

" . . . Buddy, sit your ass down and listen to me carefully," Ricky had said with fire in his voice. "I am f . . . ing tired of dealing with you, ass-hole!" With that, Ricky leaned over the table, grabbed Julian's silk necktie and yanked it. "You keep giving me the runaround. You keep putting me off. I've had enough. You haven't paid the family a damn dime of the money you owe . . . not a dime."

"Now listen to me carefully. I booked your ass on a flight to Miami on January 5th to take care of some business. Before you board the plane to Miami, a man will find you and give you a travel bag and an envelope with instructions of where to go in Miami. Do you understand? Do you understand, Mr. Frank?"

"No bullshit, you better do what I have told you . . . I know where your beautiful wife, Bridget, lives in Westport. Don't force me to hurt her." Ricky grinned, stood up from the table staring at Julian and left.

Julian could not get Ricky's demands out of his head . . . they kept coming back again and again. Julian made a horrible mistake. He had threatened the Gambino family. It was a cardinal mistake, he now realized. When Ricky met him earlier and wanted money . . . Julian snapped back at Ricky, and threatened to rat on the Family. He told Ricky if he didn't stop pressuring him for payment, he would go straight to the FBI. Now, Julian realized he was in serious trouble, for sure. It could cost him his life.

With all that swirling around in Julian's head, he felt it was time to find the terminal gate for his flight. After a short walk, he found the proper gate and went to the nearest payphone. He needed to call his legal assistant.

"I apologize Miss Jefferies for calling you at your home tonight, but I wanted to see how everything went at the office today since I was gone. Do you have a moment to talk," Julian said nervously, taking a deep breath.

"Julian, are you alright?" Miss Jefferies asked with concern.

"Yes, just been rushing around a bit," Julian answered.

"Everything went well today at the office, except that two men with the FBI dropped by this afternoon. They said they wanted to speak with you. They asked that you call them back first thing tomorrow. I told them you were out of town. Julian, what's going on? Have I done anything wrong? Should I be worried," Miss Jefferies asked in a quizzical voice.

"No Miss Jefferies, you have done nothing wrong. I don't know what the FBI wants, but I'll take care of it . . . I'll contact them tomorrow morning, I promise. My plane is about to depart . . . I've got to go." Julian hurriedly put the receiver down. He was depressed, nervous and had developed a splitting headache.

Julian slowly walked over to the National Airlines waiting area carrying the blue travel bag and found a seat in the crowded area.

"May I have your attention please ladies and gentlemen, I have an important announcement to make," blurted an airline representative through a microphone. "The scheduled departure tonight for the National Airlines flight from New York to Miami has been changed. We are sorry to announce that the Boeing 707 that was scheduled to fly to Miami tonight has been taken out of service due to a broken windshield in the cockpit. Regrettably, we are unable to have the windshield replaced in a timely manner. As a result, we are transferring all of our 105 passengers to two planes held in reserve, a Lockheed Electra and a Douglas DC-6B. The delay should take no more than an hour. We apologize for this inconvenience. Thank you for your patience."

The waiting room buzzed with chatter and some ticketed passengers became quite upset and outspoken.

An hour later, the first group of fretful passengers, all seventy-six, traveling on the Lockheed plane slowly boarded with little fan-fair. There was no order as to who flew on either plane. Within a few minutes, an airline representative announced to the rest of the travelers that they would be leaving very soon as well.

The flight announcement made Julian even more nervous as the departure time was quickly approaching. Russo had given Julian an ultimatum and he had to fly to Miami that night or else.

Just after 11:00 pm, the remaining 29 passengers, two pilots, one flight engineer and two stewardesses boarded the Douglas DC-6B, Flight 2511. The travelers were tired and showed signs of frustration. Some passengers asked why they were flying on such a small propeller plane verses a larger jet, and others voiced their dislike of the small cabin space. Julian Franks was the last to board the plane.

Earlier that evening before Julian stepped into the Douglas DC-6B for the flight to Miami, he franticly bought several large life insurance policies at the airport that were payable to his wife, Bridget. He thought if by chance, anything happened to him, he would have at least taken care of his family.

Julian starred at the blue flight bag. It was heavy and cumbersome. The object inside the bag was wrapped in duck-tape and he had no idea what it could possibly be. Julian was totally mystified. What was the rush to get to Miami this particular stormy night . . . and why the blue travel bag?

Julian knew something didn't add up . . .

VI

JUST MINUTES
BEFORE MIDNIGHT

JANUARY 5, 1960
NEW YORK, NEW YORK

"Ladies and gentlemen, this is the Captain speaking. I certainly apologize for the late departure tonight. We will be on our way momentarily, as soon as the last passengers find their seats," said Captain Dale Southerland.

Julian Frank was tired and frazzled. As he lowered his head to enter the cabin, his fear of flying started to overwhelm him. His chest tightened and his blood pressure spiked. Julian had checked his suitcase earlier, but was carrying the 20-pound blue travel bag that was handed to him right before boarding. Finding Row 7, he slid over to the window seat, crossing in front of an elderly lady on the aisle seat.

"Please excuse me," Julian said, easing into his seat.

"Certainly, take your time," the gray-headed lady responded, folding her magazine in her lap and adjusting her bifocals.

Straightening his sports coat and placing his carry-on bag under the seat in front of him, Julian buckled his seat belt and said, "So glad we are finally getting underway; we sure waited long enough."

"That's for sure; I'm worn out too," the elderly lady agreed.

"This is your Captain again. We will be leaving the gate in just a few moments. The stewardesses will be serving complimentary beverages and snacks for your enjoyment. Sit back, relax and enjoy your flight. Hopefully, you found a small pillow and blanket in your seat for your comfort. We'll be leaving this wintery New York weather and heading to sunny Miami shortly!"

Applauds erupted in the cabin.

The Douglas DC-6B aircraft that was flown that night was described as a sturdy, trustworthy airplane that met all federal aviation regulations. It had "dense" seating for economy-class, with two seats in each row on the left of the aisle and three on the right, a total of 94. The plane had four Pratt and Whitney 2,400-hp piston engines. Its cruising speed was normally set at 300 miles per hour, and had accumulated 24,836 hours of flight time. Captain Southerland was an old-timer who had logged over 16,000 hours as a pilot and he had primarily flown a DC-6. This propeller aircraft was originally developed as a military transport in WWII, and was on the way out as a civilian passenger carrier. National Air Lines used the aircraft on an emergency basics only.

Eight minutes before midnight, Captain Southerland lined up the DC-6B on Runway 31, released the brakes and pushed the four throttles to maximum takeoff power. Thinking to himself, the captain felt comfortable about the payload in the belly of the plane. With as few passengers on board, he knew the cargo bay was not full and would allow the plane greater lift.

As the plane took flight, co-pilot Jack Bates was also pleased that the airport luggage handlers had loaded the two large military green wooden crates into the cargo bay of the plane, as he had requested. The special cargo had to be on this particular flight because Bates would be paid handsomely if the wooden boxes arrived in Miami on time. It was a highly secretive mission that co-pilot Bates was involved in and no one, including Captain Southerland, knew anything about it.

The captain estimated the flight time at 4 hours, 45 minutes, taking into consideration the strong head winds and bad weather. The aircraft eventually climbed to a cruising altitude of 18,000 feet, heading south-southwest to Miami.

As Flight 2511 progressed, the weather worsened with heavy clouds. The pilot was forced to fly by instruments. He was closely monitoring the increased wind velocity and the possibility of carburetor icing.

As the aircraft leveled off, the attractive stewardesses, Marilu Odell and Valery Stuart, moved to the rear of the plane to the tiny food and beverage station. The space was quite noisy and compact.

Valery pushed the metal cart to the front of the cabin, turned, and started to work her way back down the aisle. The first person she served was a special guest, a retired military officer.

"We are honored to have you onboard tonight, Admiral."

"Thank you." He replied nodding his head.

"What would you like, Sir?"

"Bourbon and water please, and peanuts if you have them, thank you."

Two seats away, Valery passed by Roberto Hernandez, who appeared to be sleeping and she did not try to wake him. Roberto, well dressed in a dark three piece suit, was in New York for a two day international banking seminar. He was vice president of a successful Cuban bank in Havana, and had occasionally met with Fidel Castro on various banking matters. Aside from his business dealings in Havana, young Roberto had other reasons to be in the City. He had a secret meeting with a United States governmental agency about an important matter.

From the rear of the plane, Marilu began serving. The first couple she approached asked for soft drinks and cookies. As Marilu handed the drinks and snacks to the couple, she commented on the gold necklace the lady was wearing.

"Your necklace is so beautiful," Marilu said.

"Thank you! Today is our anniversary, and it was a gift from my wonderful husband, as well as our trip to Miami!"

Sitting midway in the cabin on Row 7, Marilu handed Julian a Bloody Mary as he had requested. The stewardess noticed that Frank's hand was shaking and he seemed to be a little nervous.

"Sir, are you feeling OK." Marilu asked with concern.

"Yes, I just hate flying . . . that's all."

"I totally understand. Flying in bad weather can be a little unnerving," Marilu replied, "however, the pilots are very experienced and will get us there safely, I'm sure."

"Young man, I've been going on this flight every winter to Miami for years. They are the best. Just sit back and relax . . . that drink should help," the little lady sitting beside Julian shared as she turned the page of her magazine.

Momentarily, the plane experienced a jolt of turbulence and the overhead seating lights blinked yellow, warning the passengers to remain seated and buckle up.

With that, beads of perspiration began rolling down Julian's face, he slurped down the rest of the Bloody Mary and ordered another.

At that moment, the Captain came on the loud speaker. "Folks, the radar shows that we will be going through some rough weather for a while and we will experience some turbulence, but hopefully it will not last long. I will keep you posted if there are any changes. Thank you."

Julian started panicking. His fear of flying was starting to overwhelm him. His eyes were shifting back and forth, not focusing on really anything. He began breathing faster and wanting to stand up. He didn't know what to do . . . he felt trapped.

Julian could not get out of his head the blue travel bag that he was forced to carry on board and the instructions that followed. Julian had a hard time understanding any of it. His mind kept jumping around from thoughts of his dear family, to the FBI inquiry and, of course, to insane demands from Russo. Julian was shaken to the core.

"Sir, are you OK?" asked the lady beside him.

"I feel nauseous, sick," Julian said painfully.

Julian Frank was sweating profusely now and feeling really bad. He had shortness of breath and pain running down his left arm. Julian started looking around to see if he could make a quick run to the lavatory. No one was blocking the passage to the front of the plane and the green light was on.

Julian grabbed the blue travel bag stowed under the seat, eased to the aisle and then made his way to the lavatory. He struggled to flip the latch on the lavatory door and collapsed on the tiny seat. Julian was completely exhausted and wanted to be by himself... he was really scared. He hoped that the turbulence would calm down and his anxiety would go away. He sat with his head bowed, starring at the blue travel bag.

At the same time, Valery stepped into the cockpit to alert the captain about a passenger's behavior.

"A gentleman seems quite ill and out of sorts."

"Valery, hopefully the turbulence will settle down, and the poor fellow can get some rest," Captain Southerland said smiling as he kept his eyes on the controls and his hands gripping the levers. "The good news is that we have just passed over Wilmington, North Carolina, and will shortly be heading out over the Atlantic Ocean... Just two hours to Miami."

At 2:27 a.m., Flight 2511 was just south of Wilmington and reported to the National Traffic Control that all systems were good, and they had finally broken out of heavy clouds and rain.

"But Captain, the gentleman really worries me," Valery further commented as she exited the cockpit.

As she turned and approached the lavatory area, Valery spoke with a passenger standing near the bathroom facilities. "I have been waiting a little longer than usual," the lady said with her arms folded. "You might ask if whomever is in there is alright."

Valery leaned on the lavatory door and tapped lightly, "Just want to be sure you are OK." She could hear someone sick, heaving as if they were throwing up.

At that split second, a loud blast from the lavatory rocked the plane, and the captain's instrument panel began lighting up as buzzers sounded, indicating that the number three engine was malfunctioning and on fire. Captain Southerland immediately shut the distressed engine down. Thinking quickly, he put the aircraft in a hard right turn to head back toward the Wilmington airport that they had just passed.

Valery and Marilu franticly ran through the passenger cabin and alerted the passengers to buckle-up, put their life preservers on as quickly as possible, and stay calm!

All at once at 2:33 a.m., the airliner's nose pitched downward, then the cabin went black . . .

VII

WOODBRIDGE PLANTATION

JANUARY 6, 1960
BRUNSWICK COUNTY, NORTH CAROLINA

"What the hell was that?" shouted Jay Richardson as he sat up in bed speaking to Jackie who was sound asleep beside him. Jay first thought that he was hearing a huge aircraft engine throttling up and down in the distance. Immediately following those weird sounds, he heard a loud blast or explosion that sent a bright flash of light through their bedroom window.

"Jay . . . Jay what's going on?" Jackie asked as she pulled the covers back and rolled over in bed.

"Must be those crazy Camp Lejeune Marines playing war games in the middle of the night again. Maybe a misfired rocket or a distressed military plane that has gone astray," Jay guessed shaking his head and rubbing his eyes.

"In the middle of the night! Jay, it's after 2 o'clock in the morning!"

"Oh, I know ... Thankfully, it has quietened down for now ... Say, let's get some sleep."

Just down the county road about a quarter of a mile from Jay's plantation, another famer, Richard Randolph, and his family were jolted out of bed.

"Lord, what in the world is going on ... it's going to hit the house ... I know it's going to hit the house!" Letzie, Richard's wife shouted.

Richard jumped out of bed in all the commotion, and listened with intensity to the sounds in the distance. "Honey, it sounds like huge engines starving for fuel . . . cutting in and out," Richard exclaimed. "Did you hear that explosion and see the bright flash of light in the sky? Wow ... that last explosion really shook the ground!"

Both Richard and Letzie ran to the window and pulled back the curtains. Through the dark rainy night they could see a bright orange flame in the distance across the fields for a short time and then it went out.

By the time the flames subsided, all six children in the Randolph family were up peering out the windows as well.

"What is it, what is it dad?" the children said almost in unison.

"From the sounds of it kids, it was probably something to do with the military, maybe a rocket, maybe a plane or something big that just fell out of the sky," Richard said so as not to alarm the children. "Those marines are always doing something over there at Camp Lejeune ... Now, ya'll go back to bed, you hear! Tomorrow morning we'll check it out. Hurry on now!"

"Letzie, let me help you back to bed ... since you are expecting, you don't need too much excitement; you need more rest," Richard said in a comforting tone.

Richard's mind was racing with concern as he stared out the window. He couldn't decide whether to head out in the rain and check out whatever the racket was outside, or just stay at home. He was torn in making a decision. If he put on his rain jacket and ventured out through the muddy fields, he could get tangled up in pieces of twisted steel and severely cut himself, or step on a live bomb and get blown up, or even worse, step in a giant crater and never return. He didn't know what he might find. If there were survivors, how could he help? On the other hand, what if it was a war game and soldiers had guns thinking he was an enemy and he could be shot dead just for lending a helping hand.

Richard felt staying home made more sense. Daylight tomorrow would be the best time to check out whatever it was, he thought. Hell, if someone outside needed help, he didn't even own a phone. So Richard headed to bed.

The Randolphs lived in a quite rural setting on a small farm in the county, northwest of Bolivia. After years of hard work saving his money, Richard acquired a little over a hundred acres of good farmland. He planted crops like peanuts and corn, but raising hogs was his main livelihood. A long line of mature loblolly pines bordered Richard's farm and joined Jay Richardson's property.

The oldest son, McArthur, didn't sleep much after what had happened in the wee hours of the morning. He was restless. He was ready to pounce out of bed just at the light of day. As the early dawn began to paint the sky a pale blue and the heavy fog covering the wet plowed fields started to rise, McArthur bolted out of the house. As he made his way to the back of the farm through the muddy fields with his heavy boots, he was bent over from exhaustion. After he got his wind back, he slowly moved up to a large piece of wreckage and just stared at the sight. He had never seen anything like it. The mass of silvery metal was as long as a small bus, bent and twisted. He knew it was some type of plane, but he could not believe how it was ripped open. Scattered across the field were clothes, suitcases, all kind of things . . . and even bodies. It looked like a horror film to him.

"Hey . . . Hey," McArthur yelled waving his hands. "Can anybody hear me?" He just stood there and stared. There was a strange stillness in the air. As McArthur started to move away from the wreckage, he tripped on an object that was sticking out of the mud. He looked down and was horrified. It appeared what looked like a human hand had grabbed the bottom of his frayed blue jeans. Freaking him out, poor McArthur ran home as fast as his legs could carry him.

After calming McArthur down a bit after arriving home, Richard heard enough to realize that his worst fears were true. He knew it was definitely an airplane crash, a horrible crash, a crash that probably killed everyone on board. He needed to tell someone and get help as fast as possible.

Since Richard did not have a phone, he jumped into his old green Ford pickup with his son, McArthur, by his side and drove as fast as he could down the dirt road to his nearest neighbor. He knew Jay Richardson could help him; he was a good friend. Their farms joined on the far outreaches, and it only took five or so minutes to speed over to Jay's place.

"Son, just sit here in the truck; don't go anywhere. I'll be right back," Richard said nervously as he opened the old truck door with some difficulty.

Running up the flight of stairs to Jay's front door, Richard grabbed the brass knocker and pounded several times. With no answer, he pounded the brass knocker a second time. Looking through the side glass panels, he suddenly saw a light and a shadow of a person approaching the door.

"Who is it . . . who is it?" Jay shouted, wearing his white monogramed bathrobe and barefooted.

"Jay, it's Richard Randolph, your neighbor," Richard exclaimed. "I really need your help!"

Jay opened the door and greeted his friend, Richard. "What's going on? Are you all right?"

"Did you hear anything early, early this morning?" Richard inquired, almost out of breath.

"Well, since you mentioned it, I did hear a loud noise like a light-ing strike or a sonic boom maybe," Jay replied shivering, holding the door. "Do come in!"

"Jay, there's been a horrible crash! An airplane crashed in the back of my farm early this morning . . . it's really bad, I think a lot of people were killed!"

"I'll call the authorities right now, Richard, hold on!" Jay imme-diately turned and ran to make the call.

VIII

WHITEVILLE, NORTH CAROLINA

JANUARY 6, 1960

"Hurry! Hurry! Been a horrible plane crash!" Sheriff Ben Duke shouted in his phone. Jim Hughes, the local newspaper reporter, listened intensely to the alarming message.

"Jim, meet me at my office in ten minutes and you can follow me," the sheriff said hastily.

"OK sir. I'll be right there," Jim said as he quickly grabbed his Pentax camera, extra film, writing pad, coat and hat.

The Columbus County Sheriff had notified the young 25-year-old reporter just past 8 a.m. that morning. Jim had just finished Journalism school at the University of North Carolina, and was employed by *THE NEWS REGISTER* in Whiteville, North Carolina. Jim's adrenaline was pumping and he was nervous. Time was of the essence and he had to get the facts. He had only one chance to write the very best article he could. From his training, Jim knew he had the skills to investigate this disaster, no matter how atrocious. Now it was his responsibly to capture this major news story with graphic photos as soon as possible. It was Jim's first big assignment.

Light rain still persisted through the morning hours and heavy clouds hung low as Jim Hughes raced his blue Thunderbird convertible eastbound on Hwy 74/76 following Sheriff Duke. They eventually turned onto the back roads of Brunswick County that lead to the crash site along the Old Georgetown Road.

Jim walked over to Sheriff Duke standing near his patrol car with his red beacon flashing and thanked him for getting him to the scene safely. Before Jim started to head towards the crash site, Sheriff Duke told him that shortly after dawn, a local farmer had called the Wilmington Airport Authority about a commercial airliner that had crashed near his home northwest of Bolivia, North Carolina. After receiving the news, the Airport Authority immediately called off the search and rescue mission the Coast Guard and Navy had begun in hopes of finding the lost commercial airliner.

As Jim approached the disaster area, his chest tightened and he started to hyperventilate as he approached the gory scene. The magnitude of the disaster was almost too much to grasp. Surveying the muddy, wet terrain, Jim could see through the mist in the distance what he thought was litter, aircraft debris, and bodies strewn in every direction. As Jim took notes and photographs, he could hear sirens in the distance and see emergency personnel assembling. Jim moved cautiously through the mud not to step on any artifacts of any sort. As he approached a twisted piece of metal or bundle of mail or luggage, he photographed and wrote a detailed description of what he saw. For over three hours, Jim tried to get some sort of perspective of the horrible crash and the tragic loss of life.

By mid-morning, highway patrolmen, emergency and rescue vehicles from Horry County, Wilmington, Whiteville, Crescent Beach, and Southport began converging to help at the disaster area. Light rain fell as rescuers searched for bodies. The local Salvation Army along with the Red Cross set up large tents to shelter the rescuers from the inclement weather, offering coffee and donuts.

Clarence Swartz, a retired state highway patrolman, recalled: "It was a gruesome sight and one of the worst air disasters in southeastern North Carolina history. The plane was broken into several sections. People were lying on the ground, but most of them were still strapped in their seats."

The debris field covered about 20 acres, in an area a mile and half off US 17 northwest of Bolivia. A piece of the wing and most of the ripped fuselage fell in a muddy field, while the cockpit crashed in woods 50 yards away.

At the scene, National Airline personnel said the airline was 20 miles off course. There were indications it was trying to circle back towards Wilmington, in trouble, when it either disintegrated or exploded in mid-air.

FBI Agents Inness Carlson and A.C. McDonald from Wilmington arrived to help contain the holding operations and prepared for the eventual investigations.

About noon Federal Aviation Authority Inspector, Ray A. Murray of Winston-Salem, was on the scene, and action towards removal of the bodies began. Each body was minutely diagramed and photographed before removal.

As Jim Hughes walked through the debris field, he observed that guards had been stationed to stand watch over the dead and over the debris.

That morning, Jim Hughes jotted down the following observations on his small leather notepad...

"On reaching the wreckage, all sorts of personal property was spotted, a pair of shoes, pocketbooks, luggage and clothing."

"The first major part of the plane encountered was the fuselage. It was in the edge of a small field bordered by a pine thicket."

"In the thicket, small pines were dotted with yellow life jackets and white bits of cloth. Each marked a lifeless body."

"First there was a man buried in about two feet of mud. The immediate area was spattered with mud as if the body had dropped from a great height. Next there was a woman, in much the same surrounding as the man. Her body rested in a crater created by her falling body. A yellow lifejacket marked the tragedy."

"To the left, a yellow life raft billowed, fully inflated without a puncture; a strange sight where very little else was left whole."

"The bodies were all positioned as they lay there in the mud. Most of the dead had their shoes ripped from their bodies by the impact. One couple were found still in each other's arms. Some were strapped in their seats.'"

"Why were the safety belts fastened? That will have to be answered later after the investigation is completed."

"To the right, about 300 yards from the fuselage, a wing was located. In front was a gaping hole where apparently a motor had buried itself."

"The wing was battered and torn as if it had strained every metal fiber to hold the aircraft aloft but had given way to whatever force causing the crash at the last instant, pulling away whatever it could from the fuselage."

"Behind the compartment lay a fur coat, nearby the woman who had once been its proud owner."

"Beside the wreckage a man had been covered with a blanket as he sat in his seat tightly locked in by the safety belt."

"Still further to the left a man lay in the open field, a white sheet his only protection from the misting rain. Two hundred yards more, a white pillow marked the resting place of a woman."

"Two pea green long wooden crates were stuck in the mud, rope handles on one end."

"Several victims had been decapitated in the crash. Legs and arms were missing from many others."

"Overhead Marine helicopters swooped low to mark the outer fringes of the crash. Unconfirmed reports indicate a woman had been found by a timberman nearly two miles from the crash scene."

"Ambulances began to arrive to begin the task of removing the bodies."

"Officers were assigned to bodies to prevent any looting and removal of identification papers, and funeral tents were pitched to ward off the mist as bodies were removed and recovered."

"The FBI took over and organized the necessary procedure. An investigator for the CAA instructed the Marines, CAP and law officers on how to identify victims."

"Still further to the right was the pilot's compartment and part of the fuselage."

"The pilot was still in his seat, strapped in with his head lowered. His white knuckles gripping the steering wheel. His watch read 9:35 ... the same as mine ... the only thing running in the twisted and torn compartment."

"In the wreckage was the torn and battered radio that had signaled 'All Is Well.'"

After several hours of tromping through the muddy fields, Jim Hughes headed back to his car dazed and confused, not speaking to anyone.

As lawmen secured the belongings of the deceased passengers, Father John B. McGuirk of St. Mary's Roman Catholic Church in Wilmington slowly walked among the wreckage, administering last rites of the church to the dead.

By the end of the first day, searchers found 32 of the 34 bodies in the plowed fields and marshy woods where the New York to Miami flight fell. Darkness and gloomy weather had brought an end to this day of great tragedy and profound sadness.

By 3 o'clock that afternoon, Jim was back in his newspaper office finishing his first draft from his notes he had written earlier that day. His fingers were almost numb from typing on the green keys of his old manual "Royal" typewriter. His assistant in the photo-lab had developed most of his film and Jim used the photographs to help refresh his memory of the horror he witnessed.

Several hours later, Jim leaned back in his wooden captain's chair and took a deep breath. His final and twice revised article was ready for the editor to review, approve and send to press. Words could not adequately tell the real story of what he had experienced that day, but his exceptional black and white photos gave a better image of the gory tragedy.

"Jim, you did an outstanding job on the airline article," Lee Turner, owner of *THE NEWS REGISTER*, said looking at Jim with great pride.

"Thank you, Sir. I saw things today that I would never have imagined . . . so horrifying; so graphic. I will never forget walking up to the side of the plane's fuselage and seeing humans strapped in their seats, heads bowed . . . lifeless, frozen in time," Jim said in a soft voice staring up at Mr. Turner.

"I'm sure it's something you'll never forget. Son, you've had a very long day. Why don't you head home and get some rest. I'll make sure your article gets priority in the pressroom," Lee assured Jim as he walked out of his office.

As *THE NEWS REGISTER* pressroom began to run Jim's lead story for their local paper, *THE ASSOCIATED PRESS* picked up the article on the national wire service. The riveting story of the National Airlines Flight 2511 crash was now being transmitted nationwide.

Something that Jim Hughes did not mention to Mr. Turner or anyone else about the airline crash was that there were several photographs that greatly concerned him. At the moment he took them, he did not think twice about it. He snapped every image he possibly could at the time ... hundreds of photos. Now, after much thought, he felt it best that the photographs in question be locked in his desk drawer for safekeeping. In his opinion, these photos could be the key to the cause of the crash. He wanted to protect himself as well as his employer, *THE NEWS REGISTER.*

As a young aspiring newspaper reporter, Jim Hughes wondered if any of the investigators with the Civil Aeronautics Board would reveal the truth of what really caused the horrible crash of Flight 2511 ... or would politics stand in their way?

IX

CRASH SITE OF NAL FLIGHT 2511

———————

JANUARY 6 – 10, 1960
BRUNSWICK COUNTY, NORTH CAROLINA

T he scene at the National Airline crash site resembled a bus-
tling military operation just 24 hours after the tragedy
occurred. A major search effort was mobilized by bringing in
the United States Marines, all 532 strong, the National Guardsmen,
the Civil Air Patrol and a detachment of 40 Marine helicopters from
the base at New River Air Station. The massive search party was called
the "biggest organized search party" in the region's history.

Several local TV crews and other news sources arrived on the
scene all during the day.

Troops combed the marshy areas and farmlands in the vicinity of
Bolivia in the steady rain. The men retrieved and delivered hundreds
of items that were part of the ill-fated plane. While these enormous
rescue efforts were being conducted, the Civil Aeronautics Board,
CAB, and many other officials including representatives from the FAA
and NAL were busy combing through the area as well. Some of the
officials worked with operations, others interviewed witnesses, a third

group studied the structure of the wreckage, and several specialist inspected the propellers and engines.

Search teams pinned numbered tags to the bodies as they were found. The exact location of each body along with a description of personal items, like jewelry, were noted on the identification tag. Then the bodies were removed by four- wheeled vehicles and taken to a holding area before moving them to a morgue.

Seventeen miles from the scene of the crash, a small high school gymnasium in Southport, North Carolina, was designated as the temporary morgue. The bodies of victims of the plane crash were placed in three rows on the polished gym floor. Their bodies were covered by blankets, and the victims' personal effects were placed in an envelope beside them. A four-man crew of FBI agents arrived to assist in the identification process of the deceased, while six local Coast Guardsmen policed the gym.

David Thompson, CAB investigator in charge, requested that persons with airplane parts or with knowledge where such parts may be found, please contact his office at the Cape Fear Hotel in Wilmington. He further announced that the CAB officials decided to reassemble the plane in a hangar at the Bluethenthal Field near Wilmington, North Carolina. Investigators would build a mock-up of the fuselage of wood and chicken wire, and the actual pieces of the plane would then be attached to the frame. The process would take two to four weeks to complete.

More airplane wreckage was being found as far away as 25 miles from the crash site. Along Kure Beach, two women found a sheet of aluminum "as big as an average end table" in their backyard. Also, Edward Casey found a 9-by-6-foot section of the DC-6B right forward fuselage in the woods outside Kure Beach while exercising his hunting dogs.

While the Marines and Guardsmen were running search missions throughout the area, local Wilmington pilots, Hall Watters and his brother, Robert, offered their assistance flying a tiny Piper Cub.

"It was just sheer luck that I saw the body," Hall Watters declared in an article in the local Wilmington paper. "I doubt seriously if the fella would have been found if it hadn't been for sheer luck."

Pilot Watters and his brother, both fish-spotters for the menhaden fleet in Southport, left Bluethenthal Field near Wilmington the morning of January 14, one week after the airline crash. First, they flew over the site of the main wreckage near Bolivia before heading to the Cape Fear River. Passing over Orton Plantation, both brothers started looking on both sides of the river banks. As they passed over islands in the middle of the river, the spotters would circle the island before heading further south. As soon as they passed Sunny Point, a military weapons facility, the brothers saw pieces of aluminum on the ground and spotted a row of three airplane seats in shallow water along the river bank.

Hall Watters radioed the airport and, in turn, the control tower radioed a Marine helicopter and the Coast Guard for help. As a rescue boat was closing in on the seats stuck in the river bank, Watters spotted seagulls swarming around an area several hundred yards to the south. It was a body lying in a watery marsh and was face-up. The body was in an area called Snow's Marsh on the west side of the Cape Fear River, almost 15 air miles from the main crash site.

As two Coast Guardsmen positioned themselves near the bloated body, a Marine helicopter hovered low enough for the rescuers to place the human remains on a retrievable basket. The only clothing on the corpse were his belt and his necktie. The mangled body had sustained significant injuries, including the amputation of both legs, some of his fingers fractured, and foreign fragments of wood, metal and paint embedded in his body. It was later reported that the injuries to the body were significantly different from and much more extensive than the other passengers.

Other debris that turned up at the marsh area were remnants of a blue nylon flight bag, a metal bottle of carbon dioxide, an oxygen bottle, a life jacket and a portion of the plane's ceiling.

The body was later identified by the New Hanover County Coroner as one of the two missing passengers from the National

Airline crash and his name was Julian Frank, an attorney from Westport, Connecticut.

Days later, the very last crash victim was finally located. The remains of a young Cuban man was found at the main crash site by the Marines after combing the area a second time. The victim's body was badly decomposed and was hidden under heavy brush. The individual was identified by the coroner as Roberto Hernandez, the Cuban banker from Havana.

A few days after the plane crash, many distraught relatives and friends arrived in Wilmington by plane, and were escorted to the crash site and later to the morgue in Southport. There was a tremendous outpouring of kindness and assistance from the surrounding community. Hotels offered free lodging; locals supplied free transportation.

John Morris, National Airlines Vice President, issued a statement about the crash of Flight 2511 . . . "NAL extends its deepest sympathy to the families, relatives and friends of the passengers and crew members. The plane which went down southwest of Wilmington Wednesday apparently disintegrated in the air from an unknown cause. The wreckage is scattered over a wide area. The plane was in good order and was in the hands of a veteran crew. There was nothing from the pilot prior to the crash that would indicate any malfunction. At the present time, CAB and FAA officials are in charge of the investigation and next of kin have been notified."

Oscar Bakke, director of the CAB Bureau of Safety, from Washington, D.C., arrived at the crash site several days later with a group of aircraft specialists. Bakke toured the crash site by Marine Corps helicopter and met with the accident investigation and safety teams. He offered his thanks to all the individuals who had worked so diligently on the massive recovery effort. He also extended special thanks to the United States Marines, National Guardsmen and Civil Air Patrol.

Before departing for Washington, Bakke announced that an official public hearing concerning the fatal crash would be held in Wilmington within four to six weeks.

X

RICHARDSON FARM

WHITEVILLE, NORTH CAROLINA

"Good morning, Jackie," Vinnie yelled into the phone just after dawn.

"Vinnie, I'm trying to sleep, please. What time is it? Are you OK?" Jackie slowly answered rubbing her eyes.

"Yes, of course . . . Been reading *THE NEW YORK TIMES* at my office . . . a damn article on the front page jumped out at me about an airline that crashed a couple of nights ago near Wilmington, North Carolina. Know anything about it, Sis?"

"Vinnie, hold on . . . I'm getting up . . . one minute, please."

Stepping out of bed and pulling the draperies back, Jackie was almost blinded by the brightness of the sun. "I'm up now and yes . . . it was a horrible crash of a commercial airline flying from New York to Miami. I can't believe you've read about it in the *TIMES*."

"Sis, as you know, since it flew from New York, I'm sure there were a lot of passengers from this area who were going to Florida to get away from this miserable cold weather up here. Damn, wish I could go to Miami for the winter!"

"Vinnie, the crash has been all over the news down here. Jay and I were at Woodbridge the night it happened and heard what we thought was a loud explosion, or boom or something. It turned out the next morning to be that very plane that crashed," Jackie said yawning, trying to wake up.

"Well, I'm glad you are OK. Sis, I'll get back with you later today . . . Got to go haul some more of that damn New York garbage! Those bastards!"

"Vinnie, please!"

After Jackie hung up, she headed downstairs to the kitchen to fix herself some coffee. Jay had just poured himself a cup as she entered the kitchen and kissed him.

"Hi Dear, you got out early this morning," Jackie said as she pulled her hair back behind her ears.

"Yes, needed to feed and check on the cattle," Jay said as he took off his cowboy hat and placed it in a chair.

"I just got off the phone with my brother, Vinnie, in Jersey and he read all about the plane crash in *THE NEW YORK TIMES* . . . can you believe it? Wow, news travels fast!" Jackie said.

"Yeah, not surprising. Being a commercial airline flying out of New York, I bet a lot of the passengers were 'snowbirds' heading to Florida for the winter. Very sad . . . can't believe it happened," Jay remarked.

"I know, my heart goes out to all those who lost love ones," Jackie responded in a low voice.

"Yes, I certainly agree," Jay said touching Jackie's arm. "If you'll start breakfast, I'll be right back after I unload several bags of feed out of my truck."

"Wonderful . . . I'll get started," Jackie replied with a big smile.

Overlooking the beautiful English garden outside their breakfast room window, Jackie and Jay could not stop talking about the airline crash. "Jay, I called my dear friend, Bridget Frank, last night after you went to bed. As you can imagine, she was so distraught over what had happened. She is still in shock. She still can't believe Julian died in that crash," Jackie said with sadness. "Jay, she cannot get any answers from the airline or the authorities. Luckily, her mother is there to help with the children."

"As I have said many times in the past, life can be very strange. One day everything is good and humming along smoothly, and the very next day the world is completely turned upside down," Jay said thinking of Bridget, shaking his head.

"Jay, as you remember, she is a dear friend of mine. We were in the same class at Princeton Day School and played tennis together. We had so much fun. She pursued her modeling career in New York while I joined the family business, as you know. I was actually in her wedding. We tried to stay in touch over the years. Julian and Bridget seemed to be the perfect couple . . . and this happens," Jackie shared.

"Has anything been said about Julian's funeral? I feel like you should go if possible," Jay suggested.

"No, Bridget mentioned that Julian's body is still at the morgue in Wilmington and the authorities will not give her an answer when his remains will be shipped to Connecticut. So, of course, his funeral is on hold," Jackie said.

Jay thanked Jackie for preparing breakfast and started to head out the door before he remembered to mention to her about Jim Hughes' visit. "Honey, Jim is dropping by later this afternoon to discuss the party at Woodbridge and a hunting trip we are planning. He said he will be here around 3 o'clock this afternoon. Will that work for you?"

"Yes, that's fine. Look forward to seeing him. Will you be here for lunch?"

"I should be. We're moving the young Hertford bull I just bought last week to another pasture this morning. He's a high-spirited fellow."

"Dear, please be careful!" Jackie said with a smile. "Those bulls can get wound-up as you know, dear!"

Mid-afternoon, Jim's blue Thunderbird pulled around the brick drive at the Richardson's home. Jay had just driven up as well and both walked to the front door. After Jackie heard the doorbell, she opened the door and greeted Jim.

"Hi Jackie," Jim said with enthusiasm as he hugged her and entered their home. "Thanks for letting me drop by for a few minutes. Wanted to go over some details about the party, and the plans for the pheasant hunt later this year."

Jackie suggested that they sit in the den and enjoy the nice fire in the fireplace.

"Jim, would you like anything to drink, like a beer . . . I'm getting one," Jay asked.

"Jay, I'll take a beer . . . the warmth of the fire sure feels good; it's a bitter cold day," Jim said.

"Jackie, what can I bring you . . ."

"Honey, I think I'll stay with my sweet iced tea, thanks," Jackie answered.

After everyone got settled, Jim said, "Thanks again for graciously hosting the Democratic Gala this year. The Democratic Committee, representing three counties, was extremely appreciative that it could be held at your beautiful plantation, Woodbridge. It should be well attended and a great fundraiser."

"Jim, do you think John Kennedy has a good chance to win the presidential election?" Jackie asked.

"We sure hope so. He's a young Massachusetts congressman, as you know, with a lot of good ideas about running this country. He's an excellent speaker and can rally a crowd. Do you like him as a presidential candidate, Jackie?" Jim asked.

"Yes, I'm certainly going to vote for him," Jackie said enthusiastically.

Over the next hour, the conversation was mainly about the plane crash. Jackie learned that Jim was one of the first on the scene that morning and his reporting was part of *THE ASSOCIATED PRESS* news story. In turn, Jay told Jim about his early morning notification by his neighbor and what he saw firsthand.

"Jim, we didn't see what you saw, but the pictures were devastating," Jay said.

"Words cannot describe what I saw that morning . . . it was surreal. I will never forget the moment I walked up to the side of the fuselage with the top ripped off and looked at the lifeless passengers strapped in their seats, with their heads bowed. They looked as if they were frozen in time. Everything was so still, so eerie . . . I just couldn't believe what I was seeing!"

As the conversation waned, Jackie stood and said, "Gentleman, excuse me. I'm going to the kitchen and visit with Blanche for a while. She is baking apple pies today and I want to help her."

"Jackie, enjoyed seeing you," Jim said smiling as he stood.

"Jim, hope Kennedy wins!" Jackie said as she said good-by. "Enjoyed the visit."

"Thanks, Jackie."

As the guys sat in front of the roaring fire with their feet propped up enjoying their beer, Jay and Jim reflected on fun times they had duck hunting in the pond, and flying out west bird hunting. There were a lot of laughs about falling in the pond with waders on in the dead of winter, and shooting hen pheasants out in Nebraska by mistake.

"Jim, thanks again for planning the trip this fall. We certainly had a great time last year, for sure. I'll mark it on my calendar."

"Certainly, Jay . . ."

"One more thing, I have read several good articles in your newspaper about the Whiteville football team. Coach Buck Jolley sure thinks highly of his team this fall. If the team stays heathy and there are no serious injuries, do you think they could take the conference title this year?"

"I've talked with Coach Jolley several times and he is very optimistic. He feels he has the team to do it."

"Jim, it would be great for the school as well as for the town of Whiteville!"

"Well, Jay . . . I guess I had best be going. I always enjoy coming out here. It is so peaceful. I love the white fencing along the pastures with the cattle grazing in the distance. It's quite a showplace," Jim said as they walked to the driveway in the front of the house where his car was parked.

"Jim, thanks . . . Jackie and I have worked hard to put it all together," Jay answered humbly. "We both get a kick out of raising cattle. They are a lot of fun."

"I read where the cattle prices are good this year," Jim committed.

"Yes, we hope the price holds. We plan to send about ten steers to market this fall," Jay answered.

"Before I leave, I wanted to mention something to you confidentially about the plane crash." Jim spoke in a soft tone making sure no one was near. "I'm convinced that there is more to it than what the investigators are telling us. I feel we will learn in time that this crash was a result of a mysterious plot to destroy the actual plane or someone on it."

"Damn, Jim . . . what in the hell do you think is going on?" Jay said surprised.

"I'm trying to figure it out . . . just keep it under wraps for now. I'll let you know," Jim said as he got in his car and drove away.

XI

WASHINGTON BUREAU

JANUARY 15, 1960
WASHINGTON, D.C.

O nly a few hours after the last passenger was found at the crash site, Senator Mike Monroney, (D-Okla.), head of the Senate Aviation Subcommittee, made a surprising announcement as reported by a staff writer with the *WASHINGTON BUREAU*, Frank Van Linden. "I am convinced from preliminary reports that the National Airline tragedy on January 6 in eastern North Carolina costing 34 lives was caused by a bomb on board, possibly a suicide. However, it is not conclusive."

The news flash was immediately broadcast to the FBI and CIA headquarters in Washington, D.C., about Senator Monroney's statement in reference to the cause of the ill-fated airplane that crashed ten days earlier. With that said, the FBI and CAB were still hard at work investigating the disaster on site in North Carolina.

"Senator, hope you are doing well today." said Allen Dulles, who was head of the CIA.

"Yes, thanks . . . Hope you are as well, Allen," Senator Monroney replied.

"Fine thanks, just don't like this wintery weather," Dulles answered. "I live outside of D.C. as you know, and between the traffic and icy roads coming into Washington, it wears me out."

"I feel the same way, Allen. Thankfully, I have an apartment close to my office and the harsh winter months don't hinder me as much," Monroney said.

"Senator, the reason I am calling you today is that I need your help on a matter that is top priority."

"What is it?" Monroney asked with curiosity.

"Well, President Eisenhower's staff contacted me earlier about the plane crash that took place in North Carolina. They read your statement that you released earlier and they would appreciate if you could help bring closure to this horrible accident as soon as possible," stated Dulles.

"Allen, I wish I could, but the investigation continues and all the evidence has not been finalized. As you know, I stated that it appears that it may be a suicide bomber acting alone, but it is not conclusive at this time. However, since the President has asked, I will gladly call a hearing as soon as possible, and get Oscar Bakke, head of the CAB Safety Division to testify. He can at least update us on what he knows so far as to what might have caused the crash," Monroney said.

"As head of the CIA, this matter is of great importance. I have read similar reports from the CAB Safety Division, and it appears to me that the crash was caused by a suicide bomber who acted alone, and nothing more," stated Dulles.

"Allen, it's only been ten days since the accident . . . aren't we rushing things a little? Wouldn't it be prudent to wait until the full report has been completed by the FBI and CAB investigators in a month or two?"

"Senator, you make a good point and I understand your reasoning. However, I have to carry out President Eisenhower's request. I will fill you in with more details later when I have a chance to meet with you in person. Thank you for your help."

"Of course, Allen, I will let you know how the meeting turns out tomorrow," Monroney answered.

"Again, thank you for jumping on this quickly," Dulles graciously replied.

By the next afternoon, the Senate Aviation Subcommittee Hearing was called to order and Oscar Bakke presented his investigative report to the committee:

"The National Airlines tragedy on January 6 near Bolivia, N.C., costing 34 lives, is still under investigation and every possible resource is being used to determine the cause of the accident. In fact, a hangar near the crash site is being used to reassemble the plane to determine the exact cause of the crash. Initially, it appears that there was some type of explosion on the right side of the plane near the lavatory area over the right wing. In addition, it is believed that the number 3 engine (located beside the fuselage on the right wing) had caught fire and lost power. With these events occurring at or about the same time, it is believed that the plane made a hard sweeping turn to the right, spun out of control, broke into several pieces in mid-air, and plunged to the earth. The debris field covered over 20 acres," Bakke testified reading his notes carefully and wiping his brow with his handkerchief.

Bakke continued... "Further investigation is focused on the possibility of an explosion either by decompression inside the plane or by an explosive force from within the fuselage that would result in the plane to crash. At this time, an airborne collision is thought to be highly unlikely by the evidence that has been gathered. However, as

I have stated earlier, the investigation is still on-going and nothing has been officially ruled out," Bakke said ending his presentation. Moments later, he began taking probing questions from the committee for more than an hour.

At the conclusion of the Senate Aviation Subcommittee Hearing, Senator Monroney authorized the release of Bakke's testimony to the press.

However, leaving the hearing room, Senator Monroney made a startling comment to the press that totally contradicted Bakke's testimony. The Senator stated that now he was more convinced than ever that Flight 2511 was caused by a lone suicide bomber who had in his possession a bomb, possibly homemade, that killed everyone on board the plane. The news media ran with the Senator's assessment of the crash . . . and virtually ignored Bakke's facts that the investigation was still ongoing.

Oscar Bakke left the meeting totally perplexed and frustrated. Bakke and his team of investigators who attended the meeting had not officially declared what caused the plane crash . . . much less that the disaster was a result of a suicide bomber. The crash investigation was far from being completed.

In Bakke's mind, why would a United States Senator rush to judgement and say what caused the disaster, when he earlier stated he felt it was necessary to wait until the investigation was completed, even if it took several months to get it done. Why did Monreney feel the urgency to make a statement so quickly after the last passenger was found? Why was President Eisenhower pressuring Senator Monroney to change his opinion on the cause of the crash and what was the government not telling the American public?

Later that day after Bakke had returned to his Washington office, he began thinking further about the meeting. Who in the government did he trust? Who would tell him the truth about why this horrible crash needed closure as soon as possible. What was going on in the government that needed to be kept quiet?

After some thought, Bakke knew without question who to call . . . of course, his old college roommate who is now a big wheel at the CIA. He had a hunch that his buddy, Bruce Buckley, might just know what was going on.

"Hi Bruce, hope you are doing well . . . I saw where the Red Skins won another tight game last week . . . did you go? Bakke asked.

"Man, it's good to hear from you, Oscar! Yes, my Red Skins have struggled all year, but they came through last week for sure. And I was lucky enough to go . . . great game!" Bruce replied with excitement. Bruce Buckley had been with the CIA for years and was one of the top investigators in the criminal division.

"Bruce, I'm trying to figure something out. Are you familiar with the recent plane crash in North Carolina, killing 34 people?" Oscar asked.

"Yea, I've heard bits and pieces about it. What a tragedy," Bruce said.

"Well, that's why I'm calling. I just got out of a Senate Aviation Hearing and I was shocked at how the chairman, Senator Monroney, acted. He kept pushing for me to say it was clear that the evidence pointed to a suicide bomber. However, I wouldn't go there... I kept telling him the investigation was still underway. We needed more time to determine what actually happened. He wouldn't listen to me and told the press the crash was caused by a suicide bomber, without question. Bruce, what's going on?" Oscar asked showing frustration.

"Well, Oscar . . . ah . . . ah . . . I'll tell you what I know, but for God's sake, please keep it off the record, OK. As you are well aware, I'm sharing very confidential stuff," Bruce stated.

"Promise . . . of course," Oscar quickly gave his assurance.

"There's a lot happening inside the agency right now. Senator Monroney is being pressured by Allen Dulles, head of the CIA, because President Eisenhower wants the investigation of this plane crash put to bed and finalized immediately. There is a lot of bad blood between the U.S. and Cuba right now . . . really bad."

"As you know Oscar, the Batista regime controlled Cuba up until Castro took over on January 1, 1959. When Batista was president, the Mafia controlled the Havana hotels, all the casinos and the narcotics trade. The American tourist flocked to Cuba to eat, drink, gamble, and play with the beautiful Latina girls. Batista was happy, as well as the gangsters. Everybody was making big bucks in Cuba back then. Plus, our federal government was supportive of Batista at that time, and even shipped him guns and ammo for his military . . . crazy as it may sound!"

"All that changed when Fidel Castro took over, everything went to hell. President Eisenhower found out that the CIA had grossly misjudged Castro as being a 'spiritual leader' who wanted a democratic form of government but, in reality, he ended up being a damn communist. The President got furious when he learned that the CIA agents assigned to Cuba were enjoying a lavish lifestyle at the Havana Country Club, and not monitoring the undercurrents of the changing Cuban political scene. Eisenhower demanded that the CIA find out what the hell was going on."

"Sounds like the old boys with the CIA were enjoying themselves . . . golfing, socializing, and living it up at the night clubs instead of finding out what the bearded rebels in the mountains were up to, as well as keeping a close tab on Batista's regime," Oscar commented.

"Oscar, you are exactly right. So within a month or two, the CIA Director, Allen Dulles, gave the orders to organize a special task force within the CIA to overthrow Castro, killing him if necessary. So the CIA implemented various acts of economic warfare and sabotage, and even flooded the island with political propaganda in hopes of derailing Castro as the self-imposed leader of Cuba. But all their efforts failed. Castro had dug in, and had a well-armed militia to protect him.

He wasn't going anywhere. Within months of taking over Cuba, Castro had executed many of his political foes in a public sports arena, even shown on local television. All during this time, south Florida was being transformed by the day. Cuban refugees from all walks of life were fleeing Cuba heading to America by the thousands. From this wave of humanity . . . Cuban professionals, business and land owners, as well as Cuban gangsters . . . were all coming ashore to Florida. As a result, Miami quickly became an international hub of organized crime and the birth of the notorious 'Cuban Mob' had formed."

"Bruce, I had no idea that our government was doing everything they could to silence Castro . . . even assassinate him if necessary," Oscar responded in surprise.

"Oscar, one more thing before I let you go . . . the most shocking aspect out of all of this is that President Eisenhower demanded that what the CIA was ordered to do against Castro was to be carried out in total secrecy . . . it was an undercover operation. The President felt it was imperative that the American public not know anything about the government's plans to oust Fidel Castro from Cuba. Everything had to be kept Top Secret!"

"Wow! It has the makings of a great James Bond movie!" Oscar said in amazement.

XII

THE NEWS REGISTER

JANUARY 24, 1960
WHITEVILLE, NORTH CAROLINA

Jim Hughes could not sleep the night before, and arrived at his newspaper office early that morning. He was wrestling with what could have possibly caused that horrible plane crash on January 6. Jim reached out to his boss to get his opinion.

"Mr. Turner, please come in and sit down," Jim offered as he extended his hand pointing to a chair in front of his desk.

"I really want your point of view, sir. You've been in the newspaper business for many years, and I am struggling to understand the cause of this plane crash I've been reporting on for almost three weeks. You've read my articles, and now I'm trying to make some sense out of the whole thing."

"Jim, thanks for asking. When something this tragic happens with such tremendous ramifications affecting so many families, it is worth taking time to evaluate the evidence. In my opinion, I would look at the hard cold facts as the investigators present them and study those facts closely. Then, I would step back and look at how the ongoing national and international political scene could possibly affect this crash. Was it a crash caused by a lone suicide bomber or worst… was this crash a result of a well thought-out premeditated plot to destroy one or more individuals?" Lee Turner said in a serious tone. "Jim, there is a lot going on now in our government that the average American doesn't know, and it's not good."

"Mr. Turner, I will certainly take your advice. I just feel there are a lot more factors involved in what went on before the plane ever left the runway," Jim stated in a convincing manner. "That's my gut feeling."

"You may be on to something, Jim. I have reason to think you might be right. As you know, this year is an election year and it appears that Richard Nixon will face off against the young Democratic Senator John F. Kennedy. For the last four years, President Dwight Eisenhower has been busy dealing with numerous foreign affairs, especially the latest developments in Cuba. For years, Cuba has been under the dictatorship of Batista who was ruthless and controlled everything…the military, the media and the economy. Batista got rich allowing the casinos and hotels in Cuba to be run by the American Mafia, while the average Cuban suffered. However, all this changed in Cuba the start of 1959. With Batista's abrupt departure, the bearded Fidel Castro dressed in green military fatigues marched down from the mountains and took control of Cuba with vengeance. Killing hundreds of his detractors and implementing strict communist rule, Castro became a great concern to the United States. As you can imagine, President Eisenhower has had his hands full dealing with Cuba his last year in office, and so would our new President as well."

"With a crazy communist dictator right off our Florida shore, it stands to reason the United States must be on guard!" Jim stated.

"Well, last summer in Whiteville, I had the privilege of speaking with our North Carolina Senator, Sam Ervin, Jr., about various topics and Cuba came up in our conversation. As you may know, the Senator sits on the powerful Congressional Judiciary Committee in Washington, and confided in me that the Soviet Union was very much behind the Castro regime and posed a real threat to America. For that reason, President Eisenhower was secretly pushing the CIA to have Castro illuminated, believe it or not!" Turner said shaking his head.

"With that said Sir, could the conflict between the U.S. and Cuba have anything to do with the two National Airlines planes that crashed in the last two months, both with ties to Cuba. The first one, crashed in mid-November. Flight 967 disappeared over the Gulf of Mexico. Although the aircraft was lost at sea and the CAB could not determine a probable cause for the accident, it was believed that the plane was destroyed by a bomb. Supposedly, CAB hypothesized that one man gave luggage, loaded with explosives, to a passenger who carried it onboard the plane and the bomb exploded, causing the crash. Now two months later, the second National Airline plane, Flight 2511, goes down with some passengers onboard destined for Miami and Cuba. What is the likelihood that there is any connection between the two crashes and did the CIA have any involvement?" Jim said in a curious way.

"Well, we may never know . . . but one thing is for sure, I'll bet that the Central Intelligence Agency knows more than we think," Mr. Turner said frowning. "The CIA has always spent too much time and money dabbling in international affairs where they shouldn't be. It's gotten us in trouble on many occasions."

Mr. Turner stood, gathered his coat and hat, and waved good-by. "Jim, I guess I have probably said too much, but you are a smart young man. Stay on top of this thing . . . you'll figure it out!"

As the days passed, Jim took his mentor's suggestion and began reviewing all the key possibilities of the crash that had been reported. He grabbed a yellow pad and started to make a list . . .

Was it metal fatigue that might have caused the pressurized fuse-lage to rupture? Investigators found no weakening of the aluminum structure. Could it be that a broken prop blade might have cut through the fuselage causing an explosive decompression? All the blades were in place on the hubs. Maybe the cabin relief values were to blame . . . not so said the investigators.

Chasing other possible ideas, maybe there was a mid-air collision with another plane, but there was no trace of an object hitting the plane or a lightning strike. And finally, there were no reports of a fuel-vapor explosion aboard the plane or an oxygen bottle rupture. The inspectors eliminated all of these.

The mystery deepens. According to the aeronautic engineers, the engines and propellers were working properly before an explosion took place in the fuselage. However, the series of events that happened at 3.5 miles above the Cape Fear River occurred swiftly and violently. The experts believe that an explosion inside the fuselage over the right wing of the plane impacted the #3 engine causing it to catch fire, and in turn, the blast tore open a large section of the aluminum skin all the way down the right side of the plane. Moments later, the stricken plane disintegrated in mid-air as it fell through layers of clouds to its muddy grave.

With all the evidence pointing to a bomb on board the plane and investigators proving the bomb was closest to Julian Frank when it exploded, where do we go from here? Who was Julian Frank? Why would he bring a bomb on board the flight or did he? Were there others on board the flight who had something to do with this disaster? Did it just so happen that the demise of this plane was a direct result of a criminal act by Cuba against the United States? Finally, if the Mafia had anything to do with the crash, why blow up an airline with so many innocent individuals?

Jim was eager to find out the answers, but he knew he had to wait until the Official News Conference in March to begin to fill in the missing pieces to this puzzle. With that, he put the yellow pad in his top drawer that he had locked with the hidden photographs.

XIII

OFFICIAL NEWS CONFERENCE

———————

MARCH 22, 1960
THE CAPE FEAR HOTEL
WILMINGTON, NORTH CAROLINA

The day of the Official News Conference of the National Airlines crash of Flight 2511 had finally arrived. Distraught families and friends from all over New York City, as well as locations as far away as Florida and Cuba were assembling in Wilmington, North Carolina, for the much anticipated public hearing.

Jim Hughes had prepared well for this special day and was on his way to Wilmington as well. After an hour drive, Jim rolled into downtown Wilmington and noticed a crowd had gathered outside of the Cape Fear Hotel where the meeting was to be held.

A cold northern breeze was blowing across the Cape Fear River, but the sun offered a little warmth.

As Jim approached a large gathering standing outside the hotel, he spotted Jay Richardson and his wife, Jackie, near the entrance. "Hi Jim," Jay said walking up to shake his hand. "Have a good drive over?"

"Yes, very little traffic, and how are you this morning Jackie," Jim replied.

"Great, thanks . . . excited that this day has finally come," Jackie shared.

"I certainly feel the same. I hope that the investigators have more conclusive facts to share," Jim said holding his notebook and camera. "As you know, the CAB officials have been tight-lipped lately and have not given out very much information on the case at all. I'm sure there will be a lot of questions from all the extended families . . . it will be a long day."

"I'm sure you are right," Jay said as he took Jackie's hand and started walking toward the main building to find a good seat.

By 9 o'clock, the hotel ballroom was almost at capacity. Most of the two hundred seats in the massive room were quickly taken, as well as a long line had begun to form along the perimeter of the room. The setting became quite boisterous. A dozen tables were provided in front of the audience for the officials and their technical staff to sit.

More than 50 mass media representatives jammed the CAB hearing to witness firsthand the cause of the Bolivia air disaster. Newspaper, newsreel and TV photographers jockeyed for position. Countless reporters pursued the mimeographed summaries of earlier testimony relating to the fatal crash.

"Ladies and gentlemen, I sincerely thank each one of you for coming today," said Joseph Minetti, CAB board member and spokesman for the hearing.

"I would like to call this public hearing to order. I know this news conference on the National Airlines tragedy will be very painful and disturbing at times to most of you. As investigators, we will do our best to give the facts, the hard core facts, of what occurred during the early morning of January 6, 1960. We ask that you allow us time to give our findings first, and then we will open the floor for questioning. I promise we will be available to talk to each one of you today or tomorrow. You are why we are here. Now, I will call on our CAB Lead Investigator, David L. Thompson, to give his extensive report."

For three long hours, detailed facts and critical timelines of the National Airline plane crash were given by Thompson and other members of the Air Safety Inspection team. The representatives of the airline and engine manufacturers were also in attendance. The last presentation was from an officer of National Airlines giving a formal statement of remorse for the individuals who perished in the crash. The room was frozen in silence.

Following a lengthy break, the investigators found their seats in front once more, as did the sea of attendees. In the audience was Bridget Frank, Julian Frank's widow, and her attorney, David Marks. Bridget showed no emotion, and wore dark sunglasses and dressed in a long sleek black dress. Mr. Marks and Mrs. Frank sat together in the mid-section of the seating area unnoticed.

Marks listened intently to the earlier testimony as details of the bomb pointed to the location of where Julian Frank was seated on the plane. The investigators revealed that fragments of the explosion were later found in Frank's amputated legs and mangled hands. However, the investigators never mentioned investigating other individuals on the plane, but focused primarily on a bomb that exploded near Julian Frank. To tilt more blame toward Frank, investigators questioned why he secured over a million dollars of life insurance shortly before his flight, payable to his wife, Bridget.

Holding back tears, Bridget stared at the investigators all through the hearing with a stern expression as they tried to make the case that the bombing was solely tied to her husband, Julian Frank. She never spoke a word.

To start the afternoon session, Joseph Minetti stood and slowly moved to the podium. He paused and took a deep breath. As he looked out into the audience, he could sense the tension in the crowd. At that time, he nervously leaned over and spoke into the microphone, officially opening the floor for questioning.

The solemn mood in the room quickly turned from a subdued audience to a fire- storm of emotions and tempers. Throughout the crowd, hands were raised and individuals stood to question many of the technical statements that the investigators had presented earlier. Confusion and misunderstanding filled the air. So many of the individuals who attended the meeting had traveled long distances and they simply wanted closure to the emotional ordeal of their love ones' tragic deaths.

By late afternoon, the intense questioning of the crowd slowed and Jim Hughes of THE NEWS REGESTER raised his hand. When he was recognized, he stood.

"Sir, as you are aware, the United States is at great odds with the communist dictator, Fidel Castro, in Cuba. You have pointed out that a bomb was on board the plane and your presentation focused only on one individual as the possible bomber, but have you carefully scrutinized others as well . . . especially, those from Cuba?" Jim asked.

"We are still going through the manifest and carefully looking into all of the passengers' backgrounds . . . including those from Cuba," said one of the investigators.

"Also sir, has a detailed list of what was in the cargo bay been made public?" Jim asked hoping for some sort of straight answer.

"Sir, all the items that were in the cargo bay have been identified and tagged . . . but at this time, the CAB investigators have chosen not to release the list to the public," the investigator said hastily, turning to find another questioner.

"Sir, when will we get that information?" Jim added, getting no response.

All through the questioning and answering part of the hearing, Bridget's attorney listened and did not make any comment to Bridget. Before the hearing came to a close, Bridget and her attorney stood and quickly exited the ballroom. A *NEW YORK TIMES* reporter who recognized Marks, approached him as he was leaving the public hearing and asked him to comment on the large life insurance policy that Frank purchased before his flight.

"Sir, it isn't unusual to purchase such a policy when you fly. Furthermore, we haven't been able to collect the life insurance that is due to my client," Marks said in answer to the reporter's question.

When the official news conference was brought to a close, Jackie leaned over to her husband, Jay, and said, "I think I recognized Bridget Frank who was sitting four or five rows behind us. I must hurry and speak to her ..."

XIV

THE CAPE FEAR HOTEL

MARCH 22, 1960
WILMINGTON, NORTH CAROLINA

Making her way through the crowd, twisting and turning, Jackie finally spotted Bridget standing with her attorney. After a long hug, Jackie and Bridget wiped away tears and held each other's hands. "Bridget, I am so glad to catch up with you. I know this hearing must be so hard on you," Jackie said with sadness.

"Yes, it is horrible . . . I can't believe how they are putting all the blame on my dear husband," Bridget replied.

"Jackie, please meet my attorney, David Marks, from New York. David, this is my dear friend, Jackie Richardson, who I've known for years."

"Glad to meet you, David, and thanks for being here with Bridget. I know it gives comfort to her that you are by her side," Jackie said with a sweet tone.

"David has been wonderful. He has given me good advice throughout this horrible nightmare," Bridget exclaimed, "I couldn't have done it without him."

"Bridget are you staying here, at the Cape Fear Hotel?"

"Yes."

"I know the two of you have a lot to discuss. I'll call you tonight," Jackie said as she hugged Bridget goodbye.

"Jackie, thanks . . . Let's talk tonight for sure."

Later that night, Jackie called Bridget. After a brief conversation, the two agreed to meet for lunch at Elijah's the next day.

Elijah's Restaurant, located on the banks of the Cape Fear River just down from the Cape Fear Hotel, was one of Wilmington's premier outdoor dining destinations. The rustic waterfront restaurant with panoramic views of the river featured a cuisine of delicious seafood caught locally.

"Jackie, thank you for inviting me for lunch. This restaurant looks fabulous. I love the beautiful view along the river," Bridget said with a big smile.

"My pleasure! Has your attorney headed back to New York?" Jackie asked.

"Yes, he caught an early flight this morning," Bridget replied.

"I was so glad to have the opportunity to meet him. You said you like seafood, so you will have a lot of choices. It's all fresh," said Jackie looking over the menu.

After the ladies ordered their meal, Jackie softly asked, "Hope you slept well last night. I know it has to be difficult."

"Yes, it has been hard . . . the children can't believe all the things that have happened. On top of losing their father, they have had a lot of other things to deal with. They're so upset, but my saving grace has been my dear mom and our close friends. I am so thankful for that," Bridget said with a passionate tone.

"Bridget, I am so sorry . . . you have been in our prayers."

"Jackie, you are such a dear friend and thank you for reaching out to me, especially while I'm in Wilmington. As I told you earlier, a nice gentleman at the airport took me to see the crash site as well as the reconstructed aircraft located at the local airport, the first day I arrived."

"I'm sure seeing the actual crash site had to be surreal."

"Yes . . . I got very emotional. It was as if I were reliving the disaster all over again."

Jackie listened intently to her good friend, as tears slid down Bridget's face.

As they chatted, they enjoyed their delicious crab cakes and ordered a slice of key lime pie for desert. During their hour and half time together, their conversation transitioned to lighter, happier times . . . school days when they played tennis together, fun college trips to the Jersey shore, and how their figures had changed over the years. The conversion helped bring Bridget out of the doldrums, if just for a little while.

After a delicious lunch, Jackie suggested that they drive to Wrightsville Beach about ten miles away to see the beautiful beach community and breathe some refreshing salt air. While they were chatting and looking at different sights, Jackie thought it might be a good time to mention to Bridget about the gala at Woodbridge.

"Bridget, I know this sounds crazy, but you ought to think about going with me Saturday to a fundraiser that Jay and I are hosting at our old plantation house that we are restoring. You will be our guest and I want you to meet Jay. Jay would love for you to attend . . . and furthermore, you need to get away. Like I said, it will be fun and relaxing. Also, you will see a side of the old South that you probably have never experienced, I promise," Jackie said with a little humor.

As Jackie was talking, Bridget's mind drifted back to the news conference about the plane crash. She remembered a young reporter standing and asking the investigators several probing questions. She wanted to meet the gentleman, and even talk with him.

"Jackie, I have a strange question. How well do you know the young reporter from Whiteville?" Bridget asked. "I don't remember his name, but I do remember he was with the newspaper from Whiteville."

"Oh Bridget, his name is Jim Hughes and he is a very good friend of Jay's. They are old hunting buddies. Matter of fact, Jim is organizing the gala. Would you like to meet him?"

"Yes. I sure would. He might be the very person who can help me better understanding what really happened the night of the crash."

"Well, I guess you have accepted my invitation!"

"Yes Jackie, I will go. Thanks!"

XV

THE DEMOCRATIC GALA

WOODBRIDGE PLANTATION
BRUNSWICK COUNTY, NORTH CARLOINA

Jackie arrived early at the Cape Fear Hotel in Wilmington to pick up Bridget for the gala at Woodbridge. Driving up to the front entrance of the hotel, Bridget was already standing outside dressed in a light blue silk blouse, long colorful skirt and holding a fashionable hat.

"Hi Bridget, so glad you are going with me today. I know you will really enjoy the outing and meet some wonderful friends of ours," Jackie said with a big smile.

"I'm really looking forward to this, Jackie. I need to step away from my troubled world, if just for a little while. Thank you so much for inviting me. You have told me so much about this incredible plantation and I can't wait to see it," Bridget shared.

After a twenty minute drive down several winding roads in rural Brunswick County, they slowed and turned off on a gravel lane canopied by large river oaks graced with Spanish moss. In the distance, an old white-washed antebellum home sat prominently at the end of the lane, surrounded by large white tents. Bridget gasped in amazement.

"Jackie, this is amazing! It is so gorgeous," Bridget exclaimed with excitement. "I feel that I have stepped back in time, experiencing the elegance of 'The Old South', as you promised."

"Bridget, I'm so glad you are here. I know we'll have a great time. Let's walk over to the house to find Jay as soon as I see a place to park," Jackie said.

"Certainly, I'm with you!" Bridget exclaimed.

As they began walking toward the big house, heads turned to see who was with Jackie. Her guest, who was tall, beautifully figured, and flowing blond hair, had the look of a model . . . which, of course, she was years before.

Jackie was all smiles and waved at several of her friends as they approached the front steps of Woodbridge. A large crowd, dressed in cocktail attire, gathered at the open bar in front of the massive white tent erected in the front yard. Everyone was having a grand time.

"Miss Jackie . . . So glad you are here . . . I will find Mr. Jay," said Blanche from the porch.

"Thank you, Blanche. Meet my friend, Bridget Frank, from Connecticut," Jackie said beaming.

"Nice to meet you, Miss Frank," Blanche said as she turned to find Jay.

Jackie took Bridget's hand and they started up the stairs. As soon as they got to the top, Jay stepped out the front door to greet them.

"Hope you had a safe drive," Jay said as he leaned over to kiss Jackie on the cheek.

"Bridget, this is my husband, Jay. Jay, this is my good friend who I have spoken of many times," Jackie said affectionately.

"Bridget, it is great to meet you and welcome. I'm so sorry about your husband. You have been in our prayers," Jay said extending his hand.

"Thank you."

"Girls, let's head over to the big tent and get something to drink!"

As the three of them moved around the crowd meeting several of the guests, the wonderful sounds of a saxophone playing in the distance set the mood for the afternoon. The temperature was in the 60's and the warmth of the bright sun gave energy to the fun day. Many of the guests did not venture far from the bar, while others walked around the manicured grounds where the gorgeous camellias and azaleas were in full bloom, radiating brilliant colors of pink, purple and reds.

A waiter dressed in formal attire appeared with refreshing Mimosas on a silver tray. Bridget, Jackie and Jay all opted for one and thanked the kind gentleman.

"Jay, I understand that you are quite an outdoorsman and enjoy quail hunting," Bridget exclaimed.

"Bridget, I do love the outdoors and hunting, for sure . . . quail hunting is my passion. We are blessed with a good habitat for Bobwhites at Woodbridge," Jay said with pride, "We raise the tiny quail chicks until they are full grown and release them in large coveys in protected areas on the farm. You will have to come down and hunt with us sometime. Jackie has gone a number of times with me and really enjoys it."

"Thanks, you are kind to offer, Jay."

As the ladies and Jay began to venture towards the white tent to sample the delicious hors d'oeuvres, Jay spotted Jim Hughes. "Jim, you sure have worked magic to get such a large crowd out today. I see a lot of new faces."

"Oh, I have to give all the credit to the Democratic Committee. They have really worked hard to put all this together. As you can see, the turnout has been great . . . and thanks again for letting us use Woodbridge," Jim replied smiling.

"It's our pleasure, Jim. I want you to meet a good friend of ours . . . Bridget Frank,"

"Ms. Frank, so glad to meet you, and thanks for attending."

"Jim, what a wonderful event to be held in such a fabulous setting," Bridget said as she extended her hand to Jim.

"Jim is an old hunting buddy of mine from Whiteville and is in the newspaper business," Jay said.

"It is an honor to meet you, Jim, and I well remember seeing you at the news conference in Wilmington . . . about the plane crash," Bridget said with a low tone to her voice.

"Ms. Frank, it was a sad day for many reasons, especially in regards to your late husband. As you know, the investigation is far from being over in my opinion," Jim shared.

"My attorney and I hope to learn more of what really happened," Bridget replied.

"Of course, I certainly feel the same," Jim answered.

"Jim, is Carolyn here?" Jackie asked.

"Yes, she is in charge of the desert caterer. I am sure you will run into her soon," Jim replied with a big smile.

After chatting for several minutes, Bridget turned and asked, "Jackie, I would love to tour the old home place."

"Of course. Let's go now; this is the perfect time," Jackie said waving at a guest.

As Jackie and Bridget entered the front door of the old two-story wooden house, Blanche joined them.

"Bridget, when Jay and I bought this place, it needed a lot of repair, but it had a good foundation and structurally, it was solid. Blanche can tell you . . . it's been quite an undertaking," Jackie said.

"Yes, it sure has . . . we have spent long hours getting this place in order," Blanche said with a sense of pride.

"As we have told Blanche a million times, we could not have done it without her help," Jackie said as she reached out for Blanche's hand.

"As you can see Bridget, we painted and sanded the gorgeous heart pine floors all through the downstairs. The house has basically four main rooms that are all about the same size . . . each with two widows, a fireplace and simple wainscoting along the walls." Jackie shared.

"I love the simplicity of the home. Your antique English furniture is beautiful, of course, and goes well with the time period of the plantation. By the way, who is the gentleman in the portrait?" Bridget inquired.

"It's Jay's maternal grandfather, William Mason, from Virginia who was a Confederate Officer in the Civil War."

"That's special," Bridget stated.

As the ladies moved through the home, they ended up in the modernized kitchen attached to the back of the house where caterers were busy making last minute preparations for all the party food.

"Jackie and Blanche, thank you for the tour! You have done an incredible job restoring this old structure into a charming plantation home," Bridget said with a winning smile.

The old two-story house at Woodbridge was built almost one hundred years ago from lumber that was cut on-sight and field stones that were used for its foundation and fireplaces. The wooden siding was of clapboard style and the roof was old cypress shakes. The only outbuilding that still remained on the property was a large rustic barn used for storing hay and boarding horses. On one side of the home place was a brick walkway that led to formal gardens filled with English boxwoods and dogwoods that Jay's mother, Julia, designed. On the opposite side of the house were massive river oaks with Spanish moss trailing off its branches.

"Bridget, let's go find Jay."

"Great idea. Do you think it's time for another Mimosa, Jackie?"

"Absolutely!"

As they stepped down from the porch and walked to the white tent, Jackie spotted Jay eating a piece of delicious coconut cake.

"Dear, this is so much fun ... excellent food, good music and lots of friends having a great time," Jackie said to Jay as she sipped her second Mimosa.

"I must say ... it's a fabulous party, my love!" Jay exclaimed.

"I can't begin to tell both of you how much I have enjoyed this wonderful gala," Bridget said with teary eyes. "You have been so kind to me. Thank you."

"Bridget, it has been our pleasure," Jackie said smiling. "You needed a fun getaway."

Before the sun slid behind the massive river oaks and the beautiful blue sky faded to a light pink, Bridget and Jackie said their goodbyes and headed back to Wilmington.

As Jackie drove into the hotel entrance, Bridget asked, "Please send me Jim Hughes's phone number. I want to call him as soon as I return to Connecticut."

"Certainly . . ."Jackie said smiling.

XVI

THE NEWS REGISTER

WHITEVILLE, NORTH CAROLINA

It was the first of April and a week had passed since the big Democratic gathering at Woodbridge and Jim Hughes, sitting in his office in Whiteville, felt that it was an appropriate time to call Bridget.

"Hi Bridget. This is Jim Hughes from Whiteville. Hope you had a safe trip home from Wilmington and are doing well," Jim said.

"Yes, thanks for your call Jim. I'm trying to get back to a regular routine after being gone, as you can imagine," Bridget replied. "Matter of fact, I had you on my to-do list to call you sometime this week."

"I decided to call you today because I wanted to get your thoughts on several ideas I have . . . is this a good time to chat?" Jim said.

"Yes, my mother has just taken the children to school and I have all morning to myself," Bridget answered.

"I know attending the news conference in Wilmington was really hard for you, but I hope going to the Saturday gala at Woodbridge lifted your spirits a little," Jim said with a compassionate tone.

"Absolutely . . . the party was wonderful. So relaxing. Everyone was so kind to me. Thank you again," Bridget said with a slight inflection in her voice. "The special time at the gala really gave me renewed energy, Jim. I have a challenge ahead of me, but I know I will get through this."

"Bridget, we were honored that you came, and wish the best for you and your children," Jim said.

"Jim, I talked with my attorney at length yesterday. He shares your thoughts that the investigation was rushed, and there are possibly other contributing factors that may have caused this airline disaster. He believes that in time, the investigation will certainly prove that," Bridget stated.

"Bridget, manner of fact, I hope to learn more today. I have a meeting scheduled with a reliable source who knows a lot about the inner workings of the CIA. This individual has obtained a lot of information from a senior aid to a U. S. Senator. It certainly appears that the federal government did not want the public to know all the different things that lead up to the demise of Flight 2511," Jim said convincingly.

"Jim, again, thank you so much for staying on top of all this. You have been a strong advocate to push for answers. I don't understand why the government wants to keep things so secretive for so long. This crash has touched so many people and still there are no confirming answers to what really happened that night," Bridget said. "Jim, please stay in touch and call anytime. Thanks."

As Jim hung up his phone, Jim's editor, Lee Turner, stepped into his office.

"Jim, you asked for me to drop by today. Is this a good time?"

"Certainly, I was just talking with Bridget Frank in Connecticut," Jim said with a pleasant smile.

"How is she doing?"

"Well, she seems to be trying to get back to some sense of normalcy. She said she is convinced, like I am, that the government is not telling the whole truth about the crash in its entirety."

"Jim, she is probably correct. The times I have talked with Senator Sam Irvin's aids about all the international crisis our country is facing now, I am told that President Eisenhower is greatly concerned, as I have shared with you before. The CIA continually reports that Russia is increasing their nuclear missile capabilities, and the United States could possibly be a target. As a result, the United States believes its biggest threat is now sitting 90 miles off the Florida coast . . . Cuba. Some intelligence reports indicate that Russia may try to eventually move some nuclear warheads to Cuba. If that ever happens, the United States will be forced to take immediate action against Cuba as well as Russia."

"Mr. Turner, I cannot imagine that Cuba would even consider letting Russia put missiles anywhere on their island. Surely, Castro is not that stupid!" Jim said.

"Well, I am told it is a possibility. Since Castro has partnered with the Soviet Union, he has become indoctrinated by communist ideology and has received a lot of needed supplies for his military. My bet, Castro welcomed any type of military support from Russia since he has such a great hatred for America. Remember, Fidel Castro's greatest fear is that the United States will eventually invade Cuba and take him out."

"One of the main reasons that Castro has been able to fend off any encroachment from the United States is that he has embedded spies in the intelligent networks of our government, mainly the CIA. From the very day Castro took over Cuba, one of his top objectives was to secure loyal informants in the United States so he would know what the CIA might be planning against him or Cuba. When the CIA finally woke up and figured this out, they were totally embarrassed."

Turner continued by proposing a profound question . . ."Jim, how could a new, poorly-funded dictatorship on a tiny Caribbean island mastermind such an efficient spy network so quickly? Still to this day, it has been a mystery. The only answer is that Castro was quite ingenuous and used his charismatic abilities to send out spies with a clear mission and rewarded them handsomely. Through his

Cuban spies, it is believed that Castro knew almost every covert activity that our federal government ever attempted!"

"It certainly appears that Fidel Castro planned well, and has always stayed one step ahead of the CIA. Do you know if the CIA ever infiltrated the Cuban government to find a way to take him down?" Jim asked.

"Well, believe it or not, the CIA tried everything they could at the time, but the CIA agents who were stationed in Havana were more than likely enjoying the good Caribbean life too much and were never able to get close to Castro. So as a result, the top Washington CIA officials panicked and extended an olive branch to the notorious underworld in Miami for help!" Turner said showing his great disbelief.

"Unbelievable! So the CIA formed a partnership with the Mafia!" Jim said in amazement. "That blows my mind!"

"Yes Jim, the CIA used their underground connections to find the most powerful Miami 'Kingpin'... a man who could get things done. The individual they were after was a very well-known mobster who had deep roots in both Cuba and south Florida, and who was well connected in the national Cosa Nostra hierarchy. Santo Trafficante, Jr. was their man."

"Santo Trafficante, Jr. was a powerful and wealthy mob boss. He projected an image as a nice, soft-spoken, partially bald older gentleman who wore black-rim glasses, but in reality, he was a ruthless Mafia figure who controlled the Miami and Cuban underworld with an iron fist. Before Castro took over Cuba, Trafficante's empire comprised of many casinos, including the famous Sans Souci Casino, and an incredible cash flow from narcotic trafficking. In the spring of 1959, Castro confiscated all of Trafficante's properties, even his casinos, and put him in jail. However, Trafficante was too smart for the Cuban guards. Within a few weeks, he dressed as a Catholic priest early one Sunday morning and walked out of prison unnoticed. Trafficante caught a flight to Miami the same day."

"As soon as Trafficante stepped off the plane in Miami, he seized control of both the anti-Castro Cuban gangsters who fled Havana, as well as the established Miami mobsters already working in the Florida area. The CIA knew the Mafia had the expertise to infiltrate Cuba and carry out their mission to remove Fidel Castro at any cost."

"Mr. Turner, you have given me a lot to think about and digest. As I sit here in my tiny office in Whiteville, I am utterly amazed at how the United States government operates, and how the American citizens do not have a clue as to what is really going on in this great country!" Jim expounded with a since of profound disappointment. "One more thing before you go Mr. T, I am beginning to feel that with all that is happening in Cuba, the horrible plane crash that I have been focusing on has got to be entangled with this Cuban crisis in some fashion . . . it has got to be!"

Lee Turner tipped his hat, smiled and left.

XVII

CAPRA'S RESTAURANT & LOUNGE

8400 BISCAYNE BLVD
MIAMI, FORIDA

"Tony, thanks for the ride . . . see you later tonight," Santo Trafficante, Jr. said as he paid the cabby and headed to the main door of Capra's. Santo, well-dressed wearing a loose gold bracelet around his right wrist and a prominent diamond ring on his little finger, was excited to be at his favorite night club.

"Welcome Mr. Trafficante," the head doorman said as he tipped his hat.

Most days around four o'clock in the afternoon, Trafficante would catch a taxi from his home on 71st street near Biscayne Bay and head to a bar or nightclub along Miami Beach. During these outings is when Santo would conduct his business affairs. Capra's, just off hotel row, was an upscale, beautifully decorated restaurant where men sported tailored suits and ladies dressed in cocktail dresses, pearls, and furs. Capra's was very popular during that era, and a favorite of the rich and famous.

Mr. Trafficante was escorted to his favorite secluded section of the smoke-filled bar where black leather chairs circled around a low mahogany table. Santo was greeted by his good friends, Norman Rothman, Johnny Roselli, Charlie Tourine, and Jack Ruby, who still had on his fedora. All of the men were old business associates of Santo's and eager to discuss a few new opportunities.

"Gentlemen, great to see all of you tonight," Santo said raising his hands with a big smile. "It's been months since we were all together."

As soon as Santo found his seat, one of his favorite waitresses came over and said, "Mr. Trafficante, the usual . . . Dewar's on the rocks?"

"Yes, beautiful," Santo said as he looked her over, smiling.

Norman Rothman, seated beside Santo, got a few laughs out of everyone when he started reminiscing about the golden days back in Cuba when the gamblers at the fabulous Tropicana Casino were in high glee and the scantily-dressed show girls were spinning around to the beautiful 'Latin Jazz' songs. He remembered the night that Nat King Cole first appeared on stage and how he stole the show.

"Santo, those were sweet times, my friend!" exclaimed Norman.

"Oh yes, I'll never forget the ruckus crowds gambling at the old Sans Souci Casino, that I once owned. There were beautiful big-breasted broads everywhere, drinking tropical rum toddies and enjoying the colorful floor shows with all the lights and glamor. For the life of me, I didn't think that our friend, President Batista, would ever leave us high and dry," Santo said with a slight anger tone in his voice. "The bastard was making millions off of us every year until that bearded communist S.O.B., Fidel Castro, kicked us all out!"

"Well gentlemen, with that said . . . I think I'll call for another drink. Any takers?" Norman said quickly, changing the subject.

"Fellows, I forgot to mention to you guys," Santo said. "When I was out in Vegas in February, I got to see the Rat Pack. They were fabulous! They were at the Sands and my buddy, Frank Sinatra, had just joined his friends Dean Martin, Joey Bishop, Peter Lawford, and Sammy Davis, Jr. Their performance brought the house down with their harmony, as well as their wild bantering!"

Jack Ruby was sitting at the end of the cocktail table and spoke up. "Fellows, thanks for inviting me. It's been a long time since I've seen you and I look forward doing some business with you guys. Most importantly, I especially love the night life . . . these hot babes are my kind of girls!" Jack said with a big smile.

"Jack, you old dog! Listen, it's important that you are here. Norman needs your help to hustle some firearms to Miami . . . it's a big deal, as you know, and it pays damn well," Santo said in a convincing tone.

"Santo, we go way back. I'm here for you, my good friend," Jack said raising his drink.

Jack Ruby was out of the Dallas area and ran several strip-clubs, and had been in the mob for years. He was a gunrunner back during the Cuban revolution in 1958 for Trafficante, and was now in Miami to offer assistance to Norman to secure shipments of military rifles and ammo from up north for a top secret CIA assignment.

"Johnny boy, you're mighty quiet tonight," Santo commented.

"Just enjoying the scenery, boss!" the suave Johnny Roselli said looking around the casino at the beautiful women parading by.

"Johnny, do you remember last December when the CIA contacted you in Chicago and you, in turn, suggested that they should get in touch with me since I knew most of the anti-Castro refugee organizers extremely well?" Santo asked.

"Yes, I sure do Santo. The CIA agents requested that you meet them at the Fontainebleau Hotel for a secret meeting at your earliest convenience. At first, you were very leery of those guys and agreed to go as long as you could have your personal body guard, Jimmy Longo, by your side," Johnny stated taking a drag off his Lucky Strike. Roselli was a strikingly handsome gangster out of Chicago, dressed in a fine tailored suit. The mobster had a lot of contacts in the CIA and had handled special assignments for them in the past.

"Johnny, I was really shocked what those lousy CIA bastards admitted to me. After numerous failed attempts to kill Fidel Castro, they wanted to team up with us . . . the damn Mafia! Can you believe those cowards admitted that? First, I thought it was some kind of a set-up.

Those slouches couldn't kill Castro themselves, so they wanted us to do their dirty work!" Santo said with a smirk as he sipped his drink and pulled out another Camel cigarette. "Well, the only reason that I would even considered helping those losers, was the simple fact that we could move back to Cuba, take possession of our stolen property, and open up our casinos once again."

"Santo, I think that makes a lot of sense. The CIA would pay for everything and offer us any intelligence information that surfaced from Cuba and we would, in turn, stockpile M1 military rifles and ammo in a warehouse near the Miami airport. In addition, we would organize the anti-Cuban refugees, aka the Cuban Mob, into a formidable criminal operation."

"Simply put, just kill Castro and move back to Cuba!" Johnny added with a wide grin.

"Well, as you remember gentlemen, all was going as planned until that damn commercial airliner crashed in North Carolina the first week of January. Our first shipment of M1 military rifles were lost in that crash and the CIA immediately shut everything down for a few months after that happened. Has anyone heard more about the crash except that a bomb exploded, just like the airliner that went down months earlier over the Gulf of Mexico?" Santo inquired.

Looking over at Charlie Tourine, Santo asked . . . "Charlie, by chance, do you know anything more about the crash since you live close to New York?"

"Matter of fact, Santo, I do," Charlie answered sitting on the edge of his seat, sipping his Jack & 7.

Old Charlie was associated with the Genovese crime family and owned Zappia's Tavern in the Down Neck community, a noted hangout for crime figures around Trenton, New Jersey. He had run-ins with the law all his life and arrests ranging from gambling, to robbery, to bribery and even worse.

"It's a long story, fellows. My buddy, Ricky Russo, who I've known for years, comes into my place fairly often. Well, about two years ago, this fellow by the name of Julian Frank calls up Ricky and needs cash

...a lot of cash. Ricky tells me that this Frank fellow was in high school with him years ago and now is a big-shot lawyer in the City. Frank is in debt up to his eyeballs and is desperate."

"So Ricky, who is a member of the Gambino family, cuts a deal with Frank. Ricky gets the Family to advance Frank the cash he needed and, in return, Frank agrees to execute any document that the Family requests. Simply put... old Frank had committed to a lucrative loan-shark operation... hook-line-and-sinker," Charlie said as he finished his drink and ordered another.

"Well... the idiot executed all the documents he was told to, but never repaid the Gambino's a cent... not a damn penny. He refused. We are talking thousands and thousands of dollars. So when Ricky put the heat on Frank's ass for payment, Frank threatened him. Frank said he was going straight to the FBI and rat on the Family. Can you believe that? Ricky was told to silence the son-of-a-bitch, and sent the old boy on a little trip... a plane trip!" Charlie said with his eyes wide open and nodding his head.

"That stupid Frank fellow had it coming to him... who in the hell steals from the Gambinos and then rats on them," Johnny added.

"You got that right!" Charlie continued. "Well, right after the news of the plane crash hit *THE NEW YORK TIMES*, Ricky was in the tavern drinking beer late the next day. Acting nervous, Ricky started talking about the horrible crash. The more he drank, the more he talked. I thought he was crazy at first. He talked about getting a friend of his to assemble a simple explosive... one stick of dynamite with a spark device and an alarm clock that could be set at a precise time. Ricky said he hired an old man he trusted from the Bronx to go to the airport, set the alarm device and then force that Frank fellow to carry it," Charlie said staring at Santo. "I can't believe that Ricky did that. Kill Frank for sure, but blow up a damn airliner... that's crazy!"

"That's absolutely insane, Charlie. All Ricky Russo had to do was put a bullet through the idiot's head, roll his ass into a 55 gallon drum and dump him in the river," Santo said shaking his head. "But let me assure you of one thing fellows, I'll bet the CIA quickly grabbed those military rifles out of the wreckage the next morning so nobody would ask any questions. If the news media had seen those military firearms, it would have been all over the news and the CIA would have a lot of explaining to do, those lousy bastards."

"Boss, I'm sure you're right," Charlie said.

As Trafficante looked up from his seat, he saw a celebrity that he knew well walking towards him. It was none other than his friend, Frank Sinatra. "Are you entertaining tonight?" Santo asked raising his hand.

"Yes . . . a little later tonight, Santo. Having a few drinks first, my friend," Frank replied.

"Frank, great performance at the Fontainebleau last month. The Miami crowd loved you and that young rock-n-roll kid you introduced that night . . . Elvis Presley."

"Boy, he sure has the moves!" Sinatra responded with a grin.

XVIII

RICHARDSON FARM

WHITEVILLE, NORTH CAROLINA

It was the middle of April and a busy time on the Richardson farm. The young calves had to be weaned from their mothers, and pastures needed to be cut and fences mended. Jay was scurrying to keep up. Will, his farm manager, was looking over the 112 acres of tobacco that had just been planted and making sure that the recent rains had not caused any damage. Proper ditching around the fields was critical.

Jackie, on the other hand, stayed close to home helping Blanche. They were busy making orange marmalade and it was no easy task. After cutting up many lemons and oranges, the citrus slices were then boiled in a large pot with several bags of sugar and water to 220 degrees until the liquid jelled. Too much heat would burn the mixture and cooking too long would make the jam too thick. Blanche was a master at it and Jackie was a fast learner. After the jam cooled, the sweet liquid was carefully poured into small jars. The final touch was pouring hot paraffin wax on the top of each jar to preserve the home-made jam. Jackie kept the special jars under the stairs in a tiny enclosure at their home and she would give the jars of marmalade as gifts to friends on special occasions. It was a wonderful tradition Julia Richardson, her mother-in-law, had shared with Jackie. A red ribbon tied around the top of the jar made a perfect gift!

Later that day after Jackie had rested from a busy morning in the kitchen, she placed a call to her father in Trenton, New Jersey. Her mother had told Jackie that he was not doing so well and that he had some news he wanted to personally share with her.

"Hi Papa, how are you doing? Mama says you aren't feeling well."

"Honey, my arthritis is giving me a fit, but that's not what's really on my mind."

"What do you mean, Papa?"

"I'm going on vacation as a gift from the government."

"Really?"

"Yes, I'm going to federal prison for a good while, baby," Vito exclaimed.

"Papa, what are you saying . . . when did all this happen? No one has mentioned a word to me about all this," Jackie said quite alarmed.

"I didn't want my baby girl to worry. It's not good news. The Feds have put together substantial evidence to prosecute me for drug trafficking. The bastards claim I'm involved in an international heroin operation and they convicted me last week," Vito said calmly.

"Papa, how can they do that to you?" Jackie said crying. "Are you really going to prison?"

"Yes baby . . . my attorney says the bastards are going to lock me up for 15 years, but we're going to appeal it. It's not over until it is over."

"Papa, I don't know what to say!"

"It's complicated. I have been framed by an asshole who hates my guts, and he has got the Feds to believe that I am the kingpin in an illegal drug trafficking operation. It's all a damn lie."

"How are Mama, Vinnie and all the kids handling all of this?"

"We're just taking it day-by-day. Everything will be fine, I promise," Vito assured his daughter who he loved dearly.

Jackie and her dad continued to talk for a long while about his health, pending imprisonment, as well as some revealing information about the horrible plane crash in January. Still emotionally upset, Jackie said goodbye and hung up the phone in tears.

Vito had the ability to project two extreme personalities. Whenever he was at home with family, Vito was a soft spoken, loving, devoted, Italian father. However, the short burly, tough guy was anything but easygoing and compassionate running his business matters. A reputed mobster, Genovese was known for his murderous temperament and was one of the most feared men in the world of organized crime. He held significant influence in a number of rackets, one of which was refuse disposal in the New York/New Jersey areas. Being a seasoned gangster, Vito ran the secretive Genovese Mafia Family with a tight rein and favored violence over diplomacy to settle disputes.

After the lengthy phone visit with her father, Jackie went out to her favorite flower garden behind her home and sat for some time. She needed time to decompress, sitting in her white wicker rocker with a glass of iced tea. The relaxing setting had a way of putting everything into proper perspective. How was she going to tell Jay about her father's imprisonment; what would his reaction be? Furthermore, what would he think about all the revelations that her father shared with her about the plane crash during their phone conversation?

Shortly after eight on Monday morning, Jackie called Jim Hughes at his newspaper office. The phone rang a long time before Jim answered.

"Hi Jim, I need to talk with you . . . it's important. Is this a good time?" Jackie asked.

"Certainly, Jackie. I just got to my office and the phone was ringing," Jim said, hurrying to sit down in his chair with his cup of hot coffee.

"Hope you had a good weekend, Jim."

"Yes, Jackie . . . went to Lake Waccamaw for a long weekend and worked on getting my boat cleaned up for the summer."

"Did you and Jay go to Woodbridge for the weekend?"

"No. We spent most of the weekend around the farm just catching up on several small projects. However, Saturday night I called my dad in New Jersey to check on him and he really surprised me about what he knew about the plane crash. I couldn't believe it!"

"What do you mean, Jackie?"

"Well . . . Papa said he talked with his close friend, Santo Trafficante, Jr., in Miami and was told some pretty revealing information. I mean things that really surprised me and I wanted to tell you since you are spearheading an effort to put the pieces of the puzzle together to determine the real cause of the plane crash."

"Jackie . . . I've got all day to talk when it comes to this investigation."

"Have you heard of the young Cuban passenger from Havana, Roberto Hernandez, who was on board the flight that night?

"Yes . . . I read his name on the plane's manifest," Jim replied.

"Well, sources say Hernandez was actually a spy for Fidel Castro. Papa says that the young banker acted also as a double agent for the CIA as well. Hernandez lived a dangerous life, but enjoyed a luxurious lifestyle. As a passenger on the doomed flight that night, the young Cuban was carrying a briefcase full of cash and several poisonous cigars that the CIA had placed in his possession. The goods were to be delivered to an undercover agent in Havana . . . for Castro's enjoyment, I'm sure!"

"Jackie, all this information makes a lot of sense. I feel that all the pieces of the puzzle relating to this horrible plane crash are beginning to come together. Actually, I have photos that I took at the crash site that day of an opened briefcase in the passenger aisle of the plane that had a lot of cash pouring out of it. The cigars, I can't validate; I didn't see those, but it makes since," Jim stated sipping his coffee. "Jackie, just remember, please keep all this under wraps . . . I haven't shared these photos with anyone."

"Of course; I totally understand," Jackie promised. "Jim, I have one more thing to share with you that really blows my mind."

"What is it?" Jim asked.

"Papa said that he had never known the CIA to align themselves with the Mafia . . . how crazy is that? Well, he went on to say that a lot of guns and ammunition were needed to mount an offensive, a future invasion, in Cuba to kill Fidel Castro, and to get it done, they contacted Johnny Roselli for help," Jackie stated. "Jim, have you heard any of this before?"

"I have read somewhere that Johnny Roselli was big in the Chicago Mafia, and had also been associated with the CIA to carry out other secret missions for them in past years. Strange bedfellows, for sure," Jim responded.

"Papa mentioned that Johnny was back in the gunrunning business again. I am told that boxes of military guns were in the cargo bay of Flight 2511 and the plane's co-pilot, Jack Bate, was working with Roselli on the side. Jim, that plane had all kinds of mysterious things going on. No wonder the government was trying to keep all this hidden from the public!"

"Matter of fact, Jackie, to prove your father's point, I have photos of those very rifles that were on board the plane. Two army-green wooden crates were broken open exposing the guns near the main fuselage of the plane when I took the pictures early that day. Again, please keep all this quiet. I am positive that the CIA does not want anyone to know that those military rifles were on that commercial flight."

"Damn, Jim. I can hardly believe all this happened! Have you spoken with Bridget about all this?" Jackie asked.

"Yes, I have shared most of this with her. She wants me to get in front of the Congressional Committee as soon as possible, and get some answers. She wants to know the truth about what caused the crash so she can move on with her life. However, she still can't accept the fact that her husband did anything wrong. She gets very upset when I mention the subject of the bomb," Jim said regrettably.

"Jim, I apologize if I sound a little wound-up. I am shocked at all this. I pray that you can piece all this information together about the crash and do something with it. The federal government needs to tell us the truth." Jackie said with frustration.

"Jackie, I think I have enough evidence to get someone's attention in Washington, and I think I have an idea as to why the Senate rushed the cover-up as well."

"That's wonderful Jim. Jay and I will support all your efforts to get this resolved. Just keep us posted," Jackie asked.

"Jackie, thanks . . . but please don't breathe a word to anyone what I have shared with you today," Jim stated with conviction.

"I promise!"

XIX

HUGHES COTTAGE

LAKE WACCAMAW, NORTH CAROLINA

Since there were no pressing news stories that had developed overnight, Jim put the top down on his convertible and headed to the lake. It was late April and a beautiful day to slip away from the office. He wanted to be alone. He needed to clear his head from his daily routines and totally focus on how he was going to lay out all the new developments that greatly affected the outcome of the horrible NAL crash in January. Jim was on a mission and had to get his thoughts together.

For an hour or two, Jim sat on the end of his pier, sipping a Budweiser and watching the seagulls dance through the afternoon sky over the lake. The cool, gentle breezes off the water made for a wonderful time to just sit and absorb nature at its finest. However, Jim knew he had one pressing phone call to make that day.

"Hi Bridget, its Jim ... how are you?" Jim said. There was silence on the other end of the phone and then she answered, crying.

"Jim, I apologize. My whole world has been turned upside down. I can't sleep; I'm a wreck!"

"Bridget ... what's going on?"

"Over the last two days, Miss Jefferies and I have been in Julian's office in New York going through files and all his papers," Bridget said crying more,"

"Bridget, let me call you later ..."

"No, I'm OK. I've discovered a letter from Julian that was in his office that has made me sick, really sick ... He's admitted doing some horrible things. Really, really bad things. I can't believe it."

"Bridget, we don't have to go through this now. You are emotionally upset and we can do this at another time," Jim pleaded.

"No Jim, I must get through this now. Please, please stay on the phone."

"Of course, Bridget; just take your time. I have all the time in the world."

"Well ... when we opened Julian's office door and walked in, it looked just the way it was the last time I visited. I sat down in one of the chairs in front of his desk and put my head in my hands. The realization of Julian's death hit me again. I was overwhelmed. Thankfully, Miss Jefferies was by my side. I took a quick glance across his large desk and credenza. Loose papers were stacked on the right corner of his desk and his phone was on the left. Nothing looked out of place. His credenza was crowded with framed pictures of our precious children and me; it told a sweet story of such a happy family during such happy times, and now everything is lost!"

"Bridget, do you need to take a break?"

"Thanks ... I think I can finish," Bridget said quietly. "At that time, I moved and sat in Julian's chair and began opening the drawers slowly. I turned to the left side, pulled open each drawer, and there were just miscellaneous items like a dictionary, random books, candy bars, writing pads, and hundreds of calling cards in binders. On the right

side, the drawers were locked. Miss Jefferies said she did not have a
key, but suggested that I look in the middle drawer. Without hesitation, I open the drawer and before me was an envelope address to me
in Julian's handwriting. I froze. I called Miss Jefferies over and pointed
at it. She acted puzzled as well. What would be in this letter? What did
he want to tell me that he couldn't tell me in person? So many questions ran through my mind," Bridget exclaimed, as her breathing
became more rapid on the phone.

Then Bridget started reading part of the letter . . .

> "My beloved, Bridget. As you read this letter, know how
> much I love you and deeply care for you. You have been
> the center of my universe and such a wonderful mother
> to our two beautiful children. However, I have failed you
> miserably as a husband and man you have trusted all
> during our marriage. My insane drive and ambitions
> were far too grand for me to ever achieve as a young
> lawyer trying to make it big in New York. I was impa-
> tient. I was stupid. I wouldn't listen to common sense."

> "So instead of facing public embarrassment of bank-
> ruptcy among my family and friends, I willfully chose to
> sell out to the underworld, to a powerful New Jersey
> Mafia family. They bank-rolled me with cash, but it
> ended up costing me my life. The Mafia made me do
> something that I feared most."

At that moment, Bridget started crying again and hung up the
phone.

Jim waited an hour and called Bridget back. She answered quickly
with a sincere apology.

"Bridget, please don't apologize. I can't imagine the shock you
have been through, the horror you are experiencing. For almost four

months, you have defended Julian to the fullest, and endured such sadness and heartbreak. And, now to discover his letter! Bridget, did you have any idea about any of this?"

"Absolutely not; not in my wildest dreams. I knew we were heavily in debt and I saw demand letters from creditors. When I would ask Julian, he would just say things were slow, but everything would work out. If I pushed him about our finances, he would get mad, so I stopped asking. However, over the last year, it appeared Julian had finally turned the corner and was on the track to become financially sound."

"Jim, when I found the desk key in the middle drawer, I opened the locked drawers to my right. That's when my world collapsed. Miss Jefferies and I were totally shocked. It was unbelievable; it was unimaginable."

"Jim, we found files after files of correspondence with a man by the name of Ricky Russo from Trenton, New Jersey. Miss Jefferies said everything in the drawers were a mystery to her. All the documents were filed by names of clients in Florida and New Jersey. The mortgage docs, according to Miss Jefferies, appeared to be formatted in a corrupt manner with excessive interest rates and illegal restrictions. The loans that Julian had prepared that were originated in Florida and New Jersey were blatantly illegal because Julian did not even have a license to practice in those states. But even worse, we found bank deposit slips to Julian's personal account from escrow accounts of clients' mortgages that had never been closed, and money that appeared to be embezzled from a large New York charity fund. And that was the tip of the iceberg. It was a day from hell . . ."

"Bridget . . . Bridget . . . you need to pull away from all this insanity, and turn the office over to Miss Jefferies and have her call the authorities. Please . . . please stay home to try to find some peace and comfort with your family and friends."

"Jim, I promise I will. Thank you for being there for me. It means so much."

"Take care and I will check on you later."

After Jim hung up, he sat in his serene setting and pondered what to make of his call to Bridget. He was shaken by Bridget's discovery, but in some ways he wasn't.

The pieces of the puzzle were beginning to come together. It was almost a perfect storm. If only Flight 2511 had not flown into a rain storm, the airplane would have been over the Atlantic Ocean when the bomb exploded and the aircraft would have crashed in the ocean. It would have been recorded in history the same as the NAL Flight 967 that crashed in the Gulf of Mexico months earlier.

If that had occurred, Julian Frank would have achieved his suicide wish by financially taking care of his family from his last minute life insurance purchases. Also, the secretive mission of the CIA would never have been revealed about the Cuban double-agent on board carrying cash and cigars to a Cuba accomplice, and the Mafia's undercover operation to hustle crates of military rifles to Miami, with the help of the plane's co-pilot, would have never been discovered... the crash of NAL Flight 2511 would forever have been an unsolved mystery!

Driving back to Whiteville late that afternoon, Jim Hughes was confident that now he finally had the answers.

XX

RANDOLPH'S RESTAURANT

---

65 WEST 54th STREET
NEW YORK, NEW YORK

"Jim, I'm so glad you agreed for all of us to meet in New York. When you said you wanted to get us together at a convenient location, I thought New York would be the most logical place to meet. I could take a train from Connecticut, and Jackie said she could come up for a visit with her family in New Jersey and drive over to Midtown," Bridget said on an earlier call to Jim several weeks before they met.

It was the middle of May and a beautiful day in the City. The sky-scrapers were gleaming with the backdrop of the bright sun and a Carolina blue sky. Earlier that day, Jim caught a flight out of Raleigh and, after landing at LaGuardia Airport, took a cab over to the restaurant that Bridget chose on 54th Street. Randolph's was a popular restaurant in Midtown, named after William Randolph Hearst, which preserved the timeless allure of the past with classic elements ranging from the rich mahogany bar and comfortable leather seating to the granite table tops. The elegant tavern, located in the famous Warwick Hotel, offered an enticing lunch and dinner selection, and a perfect setting to escape the buzz of Manhattan.

By 11:30 that morning, Bridget had arrived at Randolph's and had chosen a private seating area with a loveseat and upholstered chairs tucked in the corner of the restaurant for their luncheon meeting. Shortly after, Jim found his way to the restaurant by entering through the hotel on 54th Street.

"Bridget, I hope you had a pleasant train ride to New York today," Jim said as he placed his briefcase beside the table.

"Yes, it's always fun riding the commuter; it's so relaxing," Bridget answered as she got situated on the loveseat. "Jim, hope you had a safe flight this morning from Raleigh, as well."

"Yes. It's been a full day starting from Whiteville earlier this morning. The flight went well . . . uneventful, thankfully," Jim responded.

Minutes later, Jackie entered from the Avenue of the Americas, having driven in from her hometown in New Jersey. As Jackie approached their table, Jim and Bridget both stood and greeted her.

"So glad you are here, Jackie. How's Jay?" Bridget asked.

"Thanks for asking, Bridget. He's quite busy on the farm; it's planting season."

"Bridget, hope your children are doing well. I'm sure they're ready for summer."

"Yes, Jackie. With Mom's help, we are beginning to turn the corner and forge our new life," Bridget said shaking her head. "It's really been hard, but summer time will be good for all of us."

All were very upbeat and excited to be together. Jim summoned the waiter and ordered a round of Mimosas to celebrate the occasion of being together.

After finishing their drinks, Jim suggested that they go ahead and look over the menu and order. Within fifteen or twenty minutes, their lunch was served with a slice of lemon meringue pie, as an added surprise.

"Ladies, thanks for being here today. It's been a long, arduous journey for all three of us, but first and foremost, Bridget, we are here for you and your children. You have lost your dear husband and your children have lost their devoted father," Jim said with a tone of deep sincerity.

"From January 6, the three of us have wrestled tirelessly with the horrors of this tragedy, and fought the currents of resistance from Washington, D.C. The full, complete CAB investigation of this atrocious plane crash was never released to the American public. The very day the last passenger was found near the wreckage, members of the United States Congress immediately shut down the investigation of NAL Flight 2511, obviously for none other than political reasons."

"During my investigation, sources shared with me that President Eisenhower gave the directive to both Allen Dulles, head of the CIA, and Senator Monroney to quickly wrap up the inquiry because of the coming election between Richard Nixon and John F. Kennedy. In addition, others sources revealed that if the public had known what the CIA was really doing behind closed doors to terminate Fidel Castro, the mood of the election might have shifted, and that was what President Eisenhower was afraid of."

Handing Bridget and Jackie the typed-written summary of events that took place on Flight 2511, Jim took a deep breath and continued.

"Please read closely what I have written and feel free to suggest any changes. These are my thoughts, but you may have a better way to express the same ideas. I feel we have a very strong case to present to Congressman Monroney, and if all agree, I will go ahead and schedule an appointment with him."

As Bridget began to read the summary, she became overwhelmed with emotion; she struggled to talk. Wiping tears away from her cheeks, she slowly said...

"Again, I am heartbroken of the horrible, horrible act my husband committed. I denied it for months, as both of you know. I just couldn't imagined it was true. I am so sorry from the bottom of my heart for all the innocent people who died and what their families have had to endure . . . I don't know what else to say."

Jackie reached over and put her hand on Bridget's shoulder and said, "We are here for you, Bridget, and your children."

"Thank you."

When Jackie looked up, she saw a man at the bar not too far away staring at them with cold dark eyes. She felt like he was eavesdropping on their conversation. She thought it was quite eerie.

"Jim, let's talk a little quieter. Don't look, but I think there is someone being a little nosy and has picked up on some of our conversation," Jackie said in a subdued tone.

"Glad you noticed," Jim said.

Jackie continued, "Jim, from reading your well-written summary of the airline crash, just to confirm . . . you have the actual photos of the military M1 rifles that were in the cargo section of the plane?"

"Yes, if you flip over to the back of the document, you will find copies."

"Wow, I am shocked to read that the CIA and Mafia were actually working as one team to have Castro killed by any means possible, and the American public was shielded from knowing any of this," Bridget added.

"Exactly . . ." Jim answered.

"Also Jim, I was blown away at the section about the Cuban spy who was also a double agent for the CIA. How in the world did you find that out?"

"Bridget, please understand that I can't divulge my source, but I have a close friend in the government who is in the know."

"Well, your information is very convincing; well written. It is clear to me how you tied the suitcase of cash that you photographed to the Cuban spy, and made the logical assumption that the poisonous cigars were in his possession as well."

After Bridget's conclusive remarks, Jim continued.

"Ladies, the last point, if not the most difficult, that I have to make to the Congressman is the mystery of the bomb aboard the airliner. As we all know, the government immediately condemned Julian for his act of suicide by use of a home-made bomb. However, my investigation differs."

"Yes, Julian Frank was guilty of a crime, but he did not act alone. He had willfully gotten entangled with the New Jersey underworld from my investigation and, over time, was forced to commit many unlawful deeds. Julian eventually panicked and refused to play by the gangsters' rules. So he threatened them, and the mobsters planned his demise . . . I found this out from a direct source."

"I am convinced that the gangsters decided to play off of Julian's greatest fear of flying and forced him to take a flight to Miami. Their masterplan was to simply copy the events that took place two months earlier on an NAL flight from Cuba. That crash was as a result of an explosion onboard that ripped the plane apart over the Gulf of Mexico. Thus, the gangsters secured a home-made dynamite bomb with a timer and slipped it to Julian moments before his flight the night of January 6, but their ingenious plans failed."

"If NAL Flight 2511 departure time had not been delayed and had not experienced inclement weather during its flight, the aircraft would have been well over the Atlantic Ocean when the explosion occurred."

"Jim, that all makes sense! So, if the ill-fated airliner had gone down over the Atlantic, the military rifles and ammo that the co-pilot acquired for the Miami Mafia would never have been discovered, the suitcase of cash and cigars that the Cuban double agent working with the CIA would never have been revealed, and Julian's large life insurance policies he purchased for his family would have been paid in full," Jackie said summing up what could have actually happened.

"Yes, you are absolutely right, Jackie." At that, no one said anything until the waiter appeared with the check.

Looking down, Bridget wiped tears from her eyes.

After paying for lunch, Jim began putting his papers back into his briefcase.

"Jim, thank you for the wonderful meal and coming all the way to New York," Bridget said with a soft smile.

"Of course. It's my pleasure. I am eager to bring closure to this tragic plane crash, as we all are," Jim stated.

"Jim, I also appreciate lunch and all you have done. Thank you. You are to be commended for all the investigative work you have devoted to this case," Jackie said.

As Jackie stood and hugged Bridget goodbye, she said, "Have a safe train ride back to Newport and we will talk soon."

"Jackie, thanks for everything. You are a dear friend," Bridget responded.

"Jim, have a safe flight back home as well." Jackie said.

Shortly after, Bridget and Jim made their way to 54th Street in front of the Warwick Hotel, and caught a cab to Grand Central Station for Bridget's train ride back to her home in Newport, Connecticut. As the driver made several turns on the way to the train station on 42nd Street, he commented that a black car appeared to be following him. Hearing that, Jim and Bridget did not waste any time exiting the cab. Quickly, Jim handed the cabbie a twenty, grabbed Bridget's hand, and hurried through the train station, down the escalator to the train tracks.

The train was scheduled to depart at 3:48 and they were thirty-five minutes early. Standing along the corridor waiting for the boarding call, Jim thanked Bridget profusely for all her assistance on the investigation. He reviewed with her their next step to request a meeting with Senator Mike Monroney in Washington, D.C., who headed the Senate Aviation Subcommittee.

Shortly thereafter, the announcer called over the loud speaker for boarding of train number 8 to Connecticut. They hugged and said their goodbyes. Jim walked with Bridget down the narrow corridor to the 13th car of the train. The corridor was quite crowded.

"Have a safe trip home and hi to the children," Jim said as he watched Bridget climb aboard the train. Jim looked up and saw that Bridget had found a seat by the window. She smiled and gave him a wave. Moments later the doors of the train closed and began to ease out of the station. Jim stood and watched as the train accelerated.

A split second later, two tall men dressed in black, wearing dark glasses, walked up behind Jim and one grabbed his briefcase. Jim was startled and quickly spun around to confront the two men.

"Take your hands off my briefcase, now . . . who the hell are you?" Jim yelled. The second man stepped close to Jim and shoved a revolver into Jim's stomach.

"Come with us."

STILL TODAY, 61 YEARS LATER, THE NATIONAL AERONAUTICS BOARD INVESTIGATION OF FLIGHT 2511 HAS NEVER BEEN RESOLVED AND REMAINS OPEN!

SOURCES

BOOKS:

1. Berman, Susan, EASY STREET, New York, The Dial Press, 1981

2. Berman, Susan, LADY LAS VEGAS, The Inside Story Behind America's Neon Oasis, New York, T V Books, Inc.,1996

3. Cashill, Jack, TWA 800, The Crash, The Cover-Up, and The Conspiracy, Washington, DC, Regnery Publishing, 2016

4. Cleeton, Chanel, NEXT YEAR IN HAVANA, New York, Penguin Random House, 2018

5. Cleeton, Chanel, WHEN WE LEFT CUBA, New York, Penguin Random House, LLC, 2019

6. Deitche, Scott M., GARDEN STATE GANGLAND, New York, Rowman & Littlefield, 2018

7. Deitche, Scott M., THE SILENT DON, The Criminal Underworld of Santo Trafficante, Jr., New Jersey, Barricade Books, 2009

8. DeMille, Nelson, NIGHT FALL, New York, Hachette Book Group, Inc., 2004

9. English, T. J., HAVANA NOCTURNE, How the Mob Owned Cuba…and Then Lost It to the Revolution, New York, Harper Collins, 2007.

10. English, T. J., THE CORPORATION, An Epic Story of the Cuban American Underworld, New York, Harper Collins, 2018.

11. Gott, Richard, CUBA, A NEW HISTORY, Connecticut, Yale University Press, 2004

12. Latell, Brian, CASTRO'S SECRETS, Cuban Intelligence, The CIA and The Assassination of John F. Kennedy, New York, St. Martin's Press, 2012.

13. Negroni, Christine, THE CRASH DETECTIVES, Investigating the World's Most Mysterious Air Disasters, New York, Penguin Random House, 2016.

14. O'Neill, Tom & Piepenbring, Dan, CHAOS, 2019, New York, Little, Brown and Company, 2019

15. O'Reilly, Bill & Dugard, Martin, KILL THE MOB, New York, St. Martin's Press, 2021.

16. Perret, Geoffrey, EISENHOWER, New York, Random House, 1999

17. Raab, Selwyn, FIVE FAMILIES, America's Most Powerful Mafia Empires, New York, St. Martin Press, 2005

18. Reynolds, Nicholas, WRITER, SAILOR, SOLDIER, SPY, Ernest Hemingway's Secret Adventures, 1935-1961, New York, Harper Collins, 2017

19. Shorto, Russell, SMALLTIME, A Story of my Family and the Mob, New York, W. W. Norton & Company, Inc., 2021

20. Thomas, Evan, IKE'S BLUFF, President Eisenhower's Secret Battle to Save the World, New York, Little, Brown & Company, 2012

21. Weiner, Tim, LEGACY OF ASHES, The History of the CIA, New York, Random House, 2007

MAGAZINES, NEWSPAPERS & TELEVISION DOCUMENTARY:

1. *POPULAR SCIENCE MONTHLY*, New York, "Violent End of Flight 2511," February, 1961.

2. *THE NEWS REPORTER*, Whiteville, North Carolina, "Still Seek Two Bodies, Cause In 34 Death Airliner Crash," January 7, 1960.

3. *WILMINGTON MORNING STAR*, Wilmington, North Carolina, "Remove 32 Bodies From Wrecked Airliner That Crashed Near Bolivia," January 7, 1960. (to also include several news articles through February & March)

4. WECT Television, Wilmington, North Carolina, "Final Flight: A look at the investigation into what brought down National Airlines 2511" January 6, 2020.

This book is written in memory of the passengers and crew of National Airlines Flight 2511 who tragically lost their lives on January 6, 1960, and to their families and loved ones.